To New beginnings and
Better Day!
— ♡ — you

TO:

Kelsey

FROM:

GB.

DATE:

Experience Hope Through His Presence

Jesus Today®

Sarah Young

THOMAS NELSON
Since 1798

Published in Nashville, Tennessee, by Thomas Nelson. Thomas Nelson is a registered trademark of HarperCollins Christian Publishing, Inc.

Thomas Nelson titles may be purchased in bulk for educational, business, fund-raising, or sales promotional use. For information, please e-mail SpecialMarkets@ThomasNelson.com.

Unless otherwise noted, Scripture quotations are taken from *The Holy Bible, New International Version*®, NIV®. Copyright © 1973, 1978, 1984 by Biblica, Inc™. Used by permission of Zondervan. All rights reserved worldwide. www.zondervan.com

Other Scripture quotations are from the following sources:

The Amplified Bible: Old Testament (AMP). ©1962, 1964 by Zondervan (used by permission); and from *The Amplified Bible*: New Testament. © 1958 by the Lockman Foundation (used by permission). THE ENGLISH STANDARD VERSION (ESV). © 2001 by Crossway Bibles, a division of Good News Publishers. THE KING JAMES VERSION (KJV). THE LIVING BIBLE (TLB). © 1971. Used by permission of Tyndale House Publishers, Inc., Wheaton, Illinois 60189. All rights reserved. *The Message* (MSG) by Eugene H. Peterson. © 1993, 1994, 1995, 1996, 2000. Used by permission of NavPress Publishing Group. All rights reserved. NEW AMERICAN STANDARD BIBLE® (NASB), © The Lockman Foundation 1960, 1962, 1963, 1968, 1971, 1972, 1973, 1975, 1977, 1995. Used by permission. The NEW KING JAMES VERSION (NKJV). © 1982 by Thomas Nelson, Inc. Used by permission. All rights reserved. NEW REVISED STANDARD VERSION of the Bible (NRSV). © 1989 by the Division of Christian Education of the National Council of the Churches of Christ in the U.S.A. All rights reserved.

ISBN 978-0-7180-3469-6

Printed in China

15 16 17 18 19 TIMS 7 6 5 4 3 2 1

I dedicate this book to my nephew, Patrick Alexander Kelly. He was a young man who lived his life with a spirit of hope and courage. When Patrick was twenty-six years old, he was diagnosed with an unusual form of brain cancer. He was accepted and treated as a research patient at the National Institutes of Health in Bethesda, Maryland, and by God's grace he was given seven more years of abundant life. During those years of remission, he had great hope that cancer was now merely part of his history. So he set out on his life's course, living each day fully in God's merciful grace. At age twenty-nine, Patrick married his wife, Julie, and two years later he became a very proud father to their precious daughter, Cecilia.

When Patrick was diagnosed with a recurrence of brain cancer at age thirty-three, it was a challenge for him to hold fast to the hope of God's healing and blessing on his life. Yet he fought this new tumor with great vigor, courage, and peace. He always trusted in God's love for him and his family. Together, he and Julie would pray each night that they would respond faithfully to the difficult journey ahead. After enduring two months of rigorous chemotherapy treatments, Patrick received word that his MRI scans identified no more cancer in his brain. Family and friends rejoiced that God had yet again delivered this courageous young man from cancer's bondage. However, a month later, the cancer returned, along with sudden and severe neurological decline. On January 28, 2012, God took Patrick into his heavenly home, where he received complete, perfect healing. Patrick died peacefully, holding on to the promise of eternal hope in Jesus.

Acknowledgments

I AM BLESSED TO WORK WITH A VERY TALENTED TEAM. I owe a great debt of gratitude to Kris Bearss—my project manager, editor, and so much more! I'm thankful for Laura Minchew—my publisher who encourages me to keep writing and comes up with excellent, creative ideas. Finally, I want to thank Lisa Stilwell, senior editor of gift books, for all she does to get my books into print—and make them attractive. These women are much more than coworkers; they are valued friends.

Introduction

WRITING *JESUS TODAY* HAS BEEN A LIFE-CHANGING EXPERIENCE. I wrote it during three of the most challenging years of my life. I started working on it at a time when I thought I was too sick to begin another book. But our great God carried me through this journey and blessed me along the way with His steadfast Presence.

When my publisher inquired about what I'd learned while writing this book, the following sentence popped into my mind: *Hope shines bright in the trenches of adversity.* Let me describe the "trenches" I have been in.

Two months after I moved to Perth, Western Australia (in 2001), I came down with flu-like symptoms from which I did not recover. This was eventually diagnosed as chronic fatigue syndrome, and I lived with that diagnosis for years.

In 2008, I began to reevaluate my physical condition. There were several reasons for this. A number of people began giving me information about Lyme disease, suggesting that this might be the source of the symptoms I was struggling with. Then, in October of that year—the day after I finished writing *Jesus Lives*—I had a severe attack of vertigo. It was so sudden and so debilitating that I wondered if I'd had a stroke. This acute phase passed quickly though, and it morphed into a milder, chronic phase that has continued every day. This got my attention! Then I remembered that I'd had at least thirty to forty tick bites while living on my parents' property in Tennessee from 1999 to 2001. I had even experienced recurring flu-like symptoms during that time, but I had not suspected any connection with the tick bites. I also recalled that this family property was home to many deer—and deer ticks often transmit Lyme disease to humans.

There is very little treatment available in Australia for Lyme disease, so I began a search for doctors in the US. Quite a few people recommended a Lyme-literate physician in the Midwest. The first appointment I could get for a three-day assessment was in April 2009. I flew alone across Australia, across vast oceans and the international dateline, and midway across the US. I had to use wheelchairs in all the airports—one of my least favorite things to do. But I was on a mission: to find a way to get better.

The doctor ordered forty-two blood tests the first day I was there and a brain SPECT scan the second day. I also had many hours of consultation with her. The next day, I was back in airports—traveling to Nashville to be with family and friends. In a phone consultation a few weeks later, my doctor confirmed her diagnosis of bartonellosis (a coinfection of Lyme). She prescribed high doses of two oral antibiotics and recommended that I return to her clinic for several months of IV antibiotic treatment.

I debated long and hard about committing to this very expensive, grueling treatment program. However, the doctor had told me this would speed up and enhance my recovery, and the thought of getting well was exceedingly appealing. So I decided it was worth the investment. By this time, my husband was with me, and we drove together to the midwestern city where the doctor's clinic was located.

I had to be at the clinic, ready to receive treatment, by 6:45 every morning, seven days a week. I also had to go back to the clinic every afternoon for further IV treatment. The medicines made me feel even sicker, but this painful process was a means to an end: restoration of my health.

After I'd completed four weeks of treatment, my husband had to return to Australia, but I still had eight weeks to go. A number of Christians (and a few non-Christians) in the area reached out to me and made it possible for me to complete the twelve weeks of treatment. Some of these people—especially my host family—were heroic in their care of me, and I will never forget them.

Midway through this twelve-week protocol, the doctor told me I also had babesiosis (another coinfection of Lyme). She announced this to me cheerily, as though it were good news, but I was deeply discouraged by this discovery.

Shortly before the end of my treatment time, I received several hours of powerful prayer from some local prayer warriors. I started feeling significantly better after that, and I began taking short walks around the neighborhood where I was living. I wasn't sure whether my improvement was from the treatment, the prayer, or both; but I was thankful and encouraged. However, this improvement was short-lived. A few days after I had my last IV treatment, I relapsed. I returned to Australia in late October with a very bad cold and massive disappointment. I continued to take high doses of oral antibiotics and lots of supplements, but my health did not improve.

Once I settled back into life in Perth, I thought about doing more writing. My mind gravitated toward hope—something I desperately needed at that time. Healing continued to elude me, but I realized I could still have hope in Jesus: in His Goodness, His unfailing Love, His continual Presence. This hope gradually became my Light shining in the darkness of disappointment.

Writing was very difficult for me at that time because of severe brain fog. When it got especially bad, I would tell my husband, "I feel as if I'm on the verge of losing consciousness."

My doctor in Perth ordered some blood tests that showed I had primary hyperparathyroidism, caused by a benign tumor on one of my four parathyroid glands. To have the tumor removed using minimally invasive surgery, I had to fly all the way across Australia to Melbourne. The surgeon who treated me was very skilled, and the procedure was successful. Soon after I awoke from general anesthesia, my son in Tennessee managed to get a call through to me in my hospital room. Even with the anesthesia still very much in my body, I could honestly tell him I felt more alert than before. As a result of this surgery, the brain fog that had been holding me back was significantly reduced.

Not long after I returned to Perth, I was ready to write again. Though I still struggled with many symptoms, the Light of Jesus' hope grew brighter and brighter as I continued to write, focusing on Him. I discovered that hope is a way of seeing—a type of vision that defeats discouragement!

I am convinced that if I had been healthier, I would not have been able to write this book. I might have been able to write a different book, but I could not have written this one. *Jesus Today: Experiencing Hope Through His Presence* definitely came out of the trenches! And it is designed to speak hope into the lives of all its readers.

I believe the message of hope is extremely important at this time—for people throughout the US and around the world. Many individuals are feeling quite insecure and anxious because of economic problems, natural catastrophes, unstable governments in various parts of the world, plus nuclear and terrorist threats. There is a hopelessness creeping into people's mind-sets as they look at problems in their lives and all around them. There is also a sense of helplessness among people who have lost jobs, homes, health, or loved ones. But the hope we can find in the Bible is a sturdy reality—no matter what is happening in our lives or in the world.

For Christians, our hope is firmly anchored in the cross of Christ. Because He paid the penalty for all our sins, we know that we are fully forgiven and that ultimately our story finishes well—at the portals of heaven! Even now, as we live in the trenches of this world, we are assured that God is in control and He is good.

I refer to heaven quite a bit in this book. So I want to clarify that this glorious future is for all of us—and *only* those of us—who acknowledge our sinfulness and ask for the forgiveness Jesus secured through His finished work on the cross.

Like *Jesus Calling*, *Jesus Today* is written from the perspective of Jesus speaking to *you*, the reader. As with all my books, I relied on the help of the Holy Spirit as I worked—seeking to listen to Jesus throughout the creative process. When I write in this way, I am always selective in my listening. If anything is unbiblical, I reject it. I believe the Bible is the infallible Word of God, and I strive to present to my readers only what is consistent with that unchanging standard.

There are 150 devotional entries in *Jesus Today*, with two pages for each entry. The scriptures are all written out, as they are in *Jesus Lives*. Also, there are fifty quotations about hope (from Christian authors and the Bible) scattered throughout this book. These quotes can provide a quick "hope boost" when there is not time for in-depth reading. There is also a Scripture index at the back of the book.

I will be praying daily for all readers of this book. My desire is that *Jesus Today* will be a lifeline to people who feel as if they're sinking in hopelessness, as well as a source of encouragement to those whose lives are not so desperate. My books tend to speak to different people in different ways, meeting them right where they are. I think that's because the books help people connect with Jesus, and *He* meets us right where we are.

To Him alone be the Glory!

Sarah Young

Don't you know that day dawns after night, showers displace drought, and spring and summer follow winter? Then, have hope! Hope forever, for God will not fail you!

CHARLES SPURGEON

"See, I am doing a new thing! Now it springs up; do you not perceive it? I am making a way in the desert and streams in the wasteland."

ISAIAH 43:19

PUT YOUR HOPE IN ME, and My unfailing *Love will rest upon you*. Some of My children have forgotten how to hope. They have been disappointed so many times that they don't want to risk being let down again. So they forge ahead stoically—living mechanically. Other people put their hope in problem solving, the stock market, the lottery, and so on. But I challenge you to place your hope fully in *Me*.

No matter what is happening in your life now, your story has an amazingly happy ending. Though the way ahead may look dark to you, there is brilliant, everlasting Light at the end of your earth-journey. My finished work on the cross secured this heavenly hope for you, and it is absolutely assured. Moreover, knowing that your story finishes well can fill your present journey with Joy. The more you put your hope in Me, the more My Love-Light shines upon you—brightening your day. Remember that I am with you continually, and I Myself *am* your Hope!

*We wait in hope for the LORD; he is our help
and our shield. In him our hearts rejoice,
for we trust in his holy name. May your
unfailing love rest upon us, O LORD, even as
we put our hope in you. —Psalm 33:20–22*

*A faith and knowledge resting on
the hope of eternal life, which God,
who does not lie, promised before the
beginning of time. —Titus 1:2*

*Paul, an apostle of Jesus Christ, by the
commandment of God our Savior and the Lord
Jesus Christ, our hope. —1 Timothy 1:1 NKJV*

RELAX IN MY PRESENCE, knowing that *nothing can separate you from My Love.* The worst-case scenario in your life—that I might stop loving you—is not even in the realm of possibility. So rejoice that you don't have to perform well enough to earn My Love, *or* to keep it. This Love is pure gift, flowing out of My own perfect righteousness. It secures your connection to Me—your Savior—for all eternity.

Since the worst thing imaginable is not possible, you can relax and live *more abundantly.* When things are going well in your life, I want you to enjoy those good times fully—without worrying about what is on the road ahead. When you are facing tough times, I will help you and strengthen you with My Love. Even though you live in a world where trouble is inescapable, you can *be of good cheer* because *I have overcome the world!*

*Neither height nor depth, nor anything
else in all creation, will be able to separate
us from the love of God that is in Christ
Jesus our Lord. —Romans 8:39*

*"The thief does not come except to steal,
and to kill, and to destroy. I have come that
they may have life, and that they may have
it more abundantly." —John 10:10* NKJV

*"These things I have spoken to you, that in
Me you may have peace. In the world you will
have tribulation; but be of good cheer, I have
overcome the world." —John 16:33* NKJV

SOMETIMES MY SOVEREIGN HAND—My control over your life—places you in humbling circumstances. You feel held down, held back, and powerless to change things. You long to break free and feel in control of your life once again. Although this is an uncomfortable position, it is actually a good place to be. Your discomfort awakens you from the slumber of routine and reminds you that I am in charge of your life. It also presents you with an important choice: You can lash out at your circumstances—resenting My ways with you—or you can draw closer to Me.

When you are suffering, your need for Me is greater than ever. The more you choose to come near Me, affirming your trust in Me, the more you can find hope in *My unfailing Love*. You can even learn to *be joyful in hope* while waiting in My Presence—where Joy abounds. Persevere in trusting Me, and I will eventually *lift you up*. Meanwhile, *cast all your anxiety on Me*, knowing that *I care for you* affectionately and am watching over you continually.

Many are the woes of the wicked, but the LORD's unfailing love surrounds the man who trusts in him. —Psalm 32:10

Be joyful in hope, patient in affliction, faithful in prayer. —Romans 12:12

You will show me the path of life; in Your presence is fullness of joy; at Your right hand are pleasures forevermore. —Psalm 16:11 NKJV

Humble yourselves, therefore, under God's mighty hand, that he may lift you up in due time. Cast all your anxiety on him because he cares for you. —1 Peter 5:6–7

WHEN YOU TRUST IN ME, YOU TAKE REFUGE IN ME. So trusting Me is much more than a matter of your words; it is mainly a matter of your will. As you go through this day, you will encounter many things that can make you anxious, including some of your thoughts. If you don't stay alert, anxious feelings can slip into your day without your noticing them. When this happens, you may wonder why you suddenly start to feel bad. Usually, you just ignore those feelings. Or you may try to numb them with food, drink, television, gossip, or other distractions. How much better it is to "catch" the worry-thoughts before they take hold of you. That is why I say, *"Be on the alert!"*

If you are watchful and alert, you can choose to take refuge in Me whenever anxiety comes at you. A refuge is a place that provides protection or shelter: a safe haven. It is something you turn to for help, relief, or escape. I am eager to be your Refuge, and I am with you at all times. Nonetheless, you must exert your will by turning to Me for help. Thus, you make Me your refuge, demonstrating your trust in Me. *Blessed—happy, to be envied—is the one who takes refuge in Me.*

Be of sober spirit, be on the alert. Your adversary, the devil, prowls around like a roaring lion, seeking someone to devour. —1 Peter 5:8 NASB

Be merciful to me, O God, be merciful to me! For my soul trusts in You; and in the shadow of Your wings I will make my refuge, until these calamities have passed by. —Psalm 57:1 NKJV

O taste and see that the Lord [our God] is good! Blessed (happy, fortunate, to be envied) is the man who trusts and takes refuge in Him. —Psalm 34:8 AMP

I WILL RESTORE YOU TO HEALTH and heal your wounds. I am with you, within you, all around you—continually at work in your life. When your awareness of Me grows dim, My Presence continues to shine brightly upon you. This Light has immense healing Power. So dare to ask great things of Me, remembering who I AM. *I am able to do exceedingly abundantly above all you ask or think.* Pondering My limitless ability to help you will strengthen your faith and encourage you to pray boldly.

Praying in My Name—with perseverance—can accomplish great things. Learn from the parable of the persistent widow, who refused to give up. She kept bringing her petition to *a judge who neither feared God nor cared about men.* Eventually, her persistence wore him down, and he gave her what she sought. How much more will *I* respond to My children *who cry out to Me day and night*! Though you may have to wait a long time, do not give up. *For everyone who asks and keeps on asking receives; he who seeks and keeps on seeking finds.*

"But I will restore you to health and heal your wounds," declares the LORD, "because you are called an outcast, Zion for whom no one cares." —Jeremiah 30:17

Now to Him who is able to do exceedingly abundantly above all that we ask or think, according to the power that works in us . . . —Ephesians 3:20 NKJV

He said: "In a certain town there was a judge who neither feared God nor cared about men." . . . "And will not God bring about justice for his chosen ones, who cry out to him day and night?" —Luke 18:2, 7

"For everyone who asks and keeps on asking receives; and he who seeks and keeps on seeking finds; and to him who knocks and keeps on knocking, the door shall be opened." —Luke 11:10 AMP

LEARN TO LIVE FROM A PLACE OF RESTING IN ME. Since I—the *Prince of Peace*—am both with and within you, you can choose to live from this peaceful place of union with Me. This enables you to stay calm in the midst of stressful situations by re-centering yourself in Me. We can deal with your problems together—you and I—so there is no need to panic. However, the more difficult your circumstances, the more tempting it is for you to shift into high gear and forget My peaceful Presence.

As soon as you realize you have wandered from your place of Peace, return to Me immediately. Call upon My Name, for this reconnects you with Me and helps you feel safe. Don't be discouraged by how often you wander from Me. You are endeavoring to form a new habit, and this takes time plus persistent effort. The rewards, though, are well worth your efforts. The more you return to Me—to our resting place—the more peaceful and joyful your life will be.

For to us a child is born, to us a son is given,
and the government will be on his shoulders.
And he will be called
Wonderful Counselor,
Mighty God,
Everlasting Father,
Prince of Peace.
—Isaiah 9:6

I can do all things through Christ who
strengthens me. —Philippians 4:13 NKJV

The name of the LORD *is a strong*
tower; the righteous run to it and
are safe. —Proverbs 18:10 NKJV

Waiting with hope is very difficult, but true patience is expressed when we must even wait for hope. I will have reached the point of greatest strength once I have learned to wait for hope.

GEORGE MATHESON

*Be of good
courage, and He
shall strengthen
your heart, all
you who hope
in the* LORD.

PSALM 31:24 NKJV

I WANT YOU *TO LOVE ME, LISTEN TO MY VOICE, and hold fast to Me—for I am your Life.* This is the way of wisdom. I am training you to stay close to Me as you walk along perilous paths. In any close relationship, listening and loving are vitally important—and they are interconnected. Listen to Me as I *rejoice over you with gladness and quiet you with My Love.* Ask the Holy Spirit to help you receive My glorious Love in full measure. This will dramatically increase your love for Me.

The world is full of dangers, so it is wise to hold tightly to My hand. Listen—through My Spirit and My Word— while I talk you through tough times. *Pour out your heart to Me,* remembering that *I am your Refuge.* As you stay in dialogue with Me, I help you handle whatever is before you. *Hold fast to Me,* beloved, *for I am your Life.*

*[Choose life] that you may love the LORD
your God, listen to his voice, and hold fast
to him. For the LORD is your life, and he
will give you many years in the land he
swore to give to your fathers, Abraham,
Isaac and Jacob.* —Deuteronomy 30:20

*The LORD your God in your midst, the
Mighty One, will save; He will rejoice
over you with gladness, He will quiet you
with His love, He will rejoice over you
with singing.* —Zephaniah 3:17 NKJV

*Trust in him at all times, O people;
pour out your hearts to him, for
God is our refuge.* —Psalm 62:8

I AM THE FOUNDATION AND FOCUS OF YOUR LIFE. I AM a firm Foundation: one that will not be shaken. Before you knew Me as Savior, you had nothing to build your life upon. Every time you tried to create something meaning-ful, it would eventually collapse—like a house of cards. Without Me, everything is ultimately *"Meaningless! Meaningless!"* Ever since I became your Savior, you have been building on the Rock of My Presence. Some of the things you've worked on have flourished and others have not, but you always have *a firm place to stand*—on the foundation I've provided for you.

The key to steadiness in your life is to *set Me always before you*. When you make Me your Focus, you can walk steadily along your life-path. Many distractions will vie for your attention along the way, but *I* am the Guide who is continually before you. So keep looking ahead to Me. See Me beckoning you on—step by step by step—all the way to heaven.

"Meaningless! Meaningless!" says the Teacher. "Utterly meaningless! Everything is meaningless!" —Ecclesiastes 1:2

The LORD lives! Blessed be my Rock! Let God be exalted, the Rock of my salvation! —2 Samuel 22:47 NKJV

He lifted me out of the slimy pit, out of the mud and mire; he set my feet on a rock and gave me a firm place to stand. —Psalm 40:2

I have set the LORD always before me. Because he is at my right hand, I will not be shaken. —Psalm 16:8

Look the right way! In the world around you, there are vistas of bright beauty as well as dark, ugly waste-lands. When you look the right way—toward what is *true, noble, lovely*—you are encouraged and strengthened. I created you with a great capacity to enjoy beauty and goodness. Your soul resonates with these blessings, drawing strength from them.

As you go through this day, you will encounter things that make you cringe, things that are wrong or ugly. Deal with these as you must, but do not let them become your focus. Remember that I am with you, and listen to Me. Hear Me saying time after time, "Look the *right* way."

There is beauty not only in the visible world but also in what is unseen. This world in its fallen condition can never satisfy you fully. You yearn for perfection, and I am the fulfillment of that deep longing. I am perfect in every way, yet I am able to stay close to you as you walk through this sin-stained world. So look the right way—toward blessings, toward Me—and the Joy of My Presence will shine upon you.

Finally, brethren, whatever things are true, whatever things are noble, whatever things are just, whatever things are pure, whatever things are lovely, whatever things are of good report, if there is any virtue and if there is anything praiseworthy—meditate on these things. —Philippians 4:8 NKJV

"My sheep listen to my voice; I know them, and they follow me." —John 10:27

The LORD *make His face shine upon you, and be gracious to you. —Numbers 6:25* NKJV

You make known to me the path of life; in your presence there is fullness of joy; at your right hand are pleasures forevermore. —Psalm 16:11 ESV

TRUST ME HERE AND NOW. You are in rigorous training—on an adventurous trail designed for you alone. This path is not of your choosing, but it is My way for you. I am doing things you can't understand. That is why I say, "Trust Me!"

The jungle is thick, and you cannot clearly see what is before you, behind you, or beside you. Cling to My hand as you follow this trail in shadowy darkness. Although you cannot see Me, My Presence with you is rock-solid reality. Find hope in Me, beloved, for I am taking care of you.

Focus on enjoying Me and all that I am to you—even though your circumstances scream for resolution. Refuse to obsess about your problems and how you are going to fix them. Instead, affirm your trust in Me. Wait hopefully in My Presence, and watch to see what I will do.

Who among you fears the Lord *and obeys the word of his servant? Let him who walks in the dark, who has no light, trust in the name of the* Lord *and rely on his God. —Isaiah 50:10*

Why are you in despair, O my soul? And why have you become disturbed within me? Hope in God, for I shall again praise Him for the help of His presence. —Psalm 42:5 NASB

Therefore I will look to the Lord; *I will wait for the God of my salvation; my God will hear me. —Micah 7:7* NKJV

USE YOUR TRIALS AND TROUBLES to draw closer to Me. Whenever you start to feel distressed, turn that around by talking with Me. Let pain and problems remind you of your constant need for Me. Create a collection of brief prayers, such as: "Help me, Jesus. Fill me with Your Peace. Show me Your way." These requests are spiritual nutrients—soul vitamins. The more you use them, the healthier and happier you will be.

When you view troubles in this way—as reminders to draw near Me—you can actually rejoice in your trials. Of course, this requires training your mind to move quickly from problem mode to prayer mode. It is crucial to have your arsenal of prayers ready to use. Ask the Holy Spirit to guide you in your preparations, helping you form prayers that will flow readily out of your heart. Then practice saying them to Me until you're intimately familiar with them. When you encounter trouble of any kind, reach into your arsenal of prayers and speak one or more of them boldly. The enemy will retreat, and I will draw near.

*Teach me your way, O Lord; lead
me in a straight path because of
my oppressors. —Psalm 27:11*

*Consider it all joy, my brethren, when you
encounter various trials. —James 1:2 NASB*

*Therefore submit to God. Resist the devil
and he will flee from you. Draw near to God
and He will draw near to you. Cleanse your
hands, you sinners; and purify your hearts,
you double-minded. —James 4:7–8 NKJV*

*Let the morning bring me word of your
unfailing love, for I have put my trust in
you. Show me the way I should go, for to
you I lift up my soul. —Psalm 143:8*

12

I AM THE LORD OF PEACE. I give you Peace at all times and in every way. There is a deep, gaping hole within you that can be filled only by My peaceful Presence. People who don't know Me try to fill that emptiness in many different ways, or they simply pretend it isn't there. Even My children often fail to recognize the full extent of their need: *at all times* and in every situation. But recognizing your neediness is only half the battle. The other half is to believe I can—and will—supply all you need.

Shortly before My death, I promised Peace to My disciples—and to all who would become My followers. I made it clear that this is a gift: something I provide freely and lovingly. So your responsibility is to *receive* this glorious gift, acknowledging to Me not only your need but also your desire. Then wait expectantly in My Presence, ready to receive My Peace in full measure. If you like, you can express your openness by saying, "Jesus, I receive Your Peace."

Now may the Lord of peace himself give you peace at all times and in every way. The Lord be with all of you. —2 Thessalonians 3:16

My God shall supply all your need according to His riches in glory by Christ Jesus. —Philippians 4:19 NKJV

Peace I leave with you; my peace I give you. I do not give to you as the world gives. Do not let your hearts be troubled and do not be afraid. —John 14:27

A Christian . . . knows
that hope is a beam
of God, a spark
of glory, and that
nothing shall
extinguish it till
the soul be filled
with glory.

Thomas Brooks

Do not let your heart envy sinners, but always be zealous for the fear of the LORD. There is surely a future hope for you, and your hope will not be cut off.

PROVERBS 23:17–18

13

IN EVERYTHING YOU DO, PUT ME FIRST, and I will direct you and crown your efforts with success. Putting Me first sounds so simple and straightforward. But the world, the flesh, and the devil war against your efforts to do this. You can easily justify letting other things creep into the space and time you had set aside for Me. If this happens only occasionally, it is just part of being human. However, if you see it becoming a pattern in your life, watch out! Your priorities may have been gradually shifting—until I am no longer *your First Love.*

Putting Me first is not an arbitrary rule; it is the way to live vibrantly, joyfully—close to Me. It is also the way to live purposefully, letting Me direct your steps. When I am your top priority, other things fall into their proper place. So *delight yourself in Me* first and foremost. As you *walk in the Light* of My Presence, I open up the path before you—and *give you the desires of your heart.*

*In everything you do, put God first, and
he will direct you and crown your efforts
with success. —Proverbs 3:6 TLB*

*"Nevertheless I have this against you, that you
have left your first love." —Revelation 2:4 NKJV*

*Delight yourself in the LORD and he will give
you the desires of your heart. —Psalm 37:4*

*If we walk in the light as He is in the light,
we have fellowship with one another, and
the blood of Jesus Christ His Son cleanses
us from all sin. —1 John 1:7 NKJV*

14

Trust Me moment by moment. This is all I require of you, and it is sufficient to keep you standing firm in the midst of fierce spiritual battles. Just getting through each day is a victory as long as you stay in communication with Me. Search for Me in your moments. Keeping your focus on My Presence is the best protection against self-pity and depression.

I am calling you to trust Me in deep darkness. Take one step at a time, clinging to My hand for help and guidance. I am always near you, and I know exactly how much you are struggling.

Though the battle is fierce and you are weak, your resources are unlimited. My Spirit is ever ready to help you; you have only to ask. Remember that this Holy Helper is infinitely powerful *and* infinitely loving. I also am eager to help you. Call upon My Name with confident trust, for *My unfailing Love surrounds you.*

Trust in him at all times, O people;
pour out your hearts to him, for
God is our refuge. —Psalm 62:8

"And I will pray the Father, and He will
give you another Helper, that He may
abide with you forever—the Spirit of truth,
whom the world cannot receive, because it
neither sees Him nor knows Him; but you
know Him, for He dwells with you and
will be in you." —John 14:16–17 NKJV

Many are the woes of the wicked, but
the LORD's *unfailing love surrounds the*
man who trusts in him. —Psalm 32:10

15

LET *MY COMFORTS DELIGHT YOUR SOUL*. The world presents you with *a multitude of anxieties*—too numerous for you to count. Everywhere you turn, you see problems and trouble. In the midst of this mess, look to Me for help. Whisper My Name, "Jesus," thus reactivating your awareness of My Presence. Your perspective changes dramatically as My Presence comes onto the screen of your consciousness, lighting up your worldview. My comforts can soothe your troubled heart and delight your soul.

If the world were perfect, you would never experience the pleasure of receiving comfort from Me. Instead of letting problems discourage you, use them as reminders to seek Me—My Presence, My Peace, My Love. These invisible realities are available to you any time, any place, and they provide Joy that no one can take away from you. So *come to Me when you are weary and burdened*; I will provide *rest for your soul*.

*In the multitude of my anxieties
within me, Your comforts delight
my soul.* —Psalm 94:19 NKJV

*"Therefore you now have sorrow; but
I will see you again and your heart
will rejoice, and your joy no one will
take from you."* —John 16:22 NKJV

*"Come to me, all you who are weary and
burdened, and I will give you rest. Take my
yoke upon you and learn from me, for I am
gentle and humble in heart, and you will find
rest for your souls."* —Matthew 11:28–29

16

IN THIS WORLD of increasing electronic surveillance, privacy can be hard to come by. Safe places are also in short supply. So when you feel surrounded by trouble, remember this: *I am your Hiding Place.* Call out to Me, and I will *protect you from trouble.* I will even *surround you with songs of deliverance.*

One of the best ways to draw upon My strength is to sing praises to Me. I actually dwell in the praises of My people. So when problems are weighing heavily upon you, break free by worshiping Me—in songs, in shouts, even in whispers. These sacred acclamations decimate the darkness and invite Me into your awareness, brightening the atmosphere around you. Problems fade into the background while you are engaged in worshiping Me. Awareness of My Presence strengthens you and fills you with Joy.

When you praise Me in the midst of a hard day, both you and I are blessed. I come near, and I hide you *in the secret place of My Presence.*

Rescue me from my enemies, O Lord,
for I hide myself in you. —Psalm 143:9

You are my hiding place; you will protect
me from trouble and surround me with
songs of deliverance. —Psalm 32:7

You are holy, O You Who dwell in [the
holy place where] the praises of Israel
[are offered]. —Psalm 22:3 AMP

You shall hide them in the secret place of
Your presence from the plots of man; You
shall keep them secretly in a pavilion from
the strife of tongues. —Psalm 31:20 NKJV

17

MY GRACE IS SUFFICIENT FOR YOU. This grace is *enough* to get you through your toughest times. Do you believe this? It's one thing to believe it when circumstances are going your way. It's another thing altogether when you're struggling just to take the next step. Yet this is when My grace is the most precious and glorious—when you know you cannot go another step without it. Then it becomes the shining focus of your life.

I invite you to drink deeply from *the exceeding riches of My grace*—My favor, mercy, and lovingkindness. It is a free gift that opens the way for you into eternity. It also provides what you need to live *now,* in this fractured world. So come freely into My Presence and pour out your heart to Me. I do not always say yes to your petitions, but I *do* give you what you need. And I always give you Myself—My compassionate understanding, *My unfailing Love.*

Do not be ashamed of your weaknesses; boast about them! Through them you are learning to depend more on Me *so that My Power may dwell in you.*

[The Lord] has said to me, "My grace is sufficient for you, for power is perfected in weakness." Most gladly, therefore, I will rather boast about my weaknesses, so that the power of Christ may dwell in me. —2 Corinthians 12:9 NASB

[God] made us alive together with Christ . . . that in the ages to come He might show the exceeding riches of His grace in His kindness toward us in Christ Jesus. —Ephesians 2:5, 7 NKJV

"Though the mountains be shaken and the hills be removed, yet my unfailing love for you will not be shaken nor my covenant of peace be removed," says the LORD, who has compassion on you. —Isaiah 54:10

18

Keep your eyes on Me! I am with you, taking care of you in the best possible way. When you are suffering, My care may seem imperfect and inadequate. You seek relief, and I make you wait. Just remember: There are many different ways to wait, and some are much better than others. Beneficial waiting involves looking to Me continually—trusting and loving Me.

Thank Me for this time of neediness, when you must depend on Me more than usual. Do not waste this opportunity by wishing it away. Trust that I know what I'm doing—that I can bring good out of everything you encounter, everything you endure. Don't let your past or present suffering contaminate your view of the future. I am the Lord of your future, and I have good things in store for you. I alone know the things I am planning for you—*to give you a future and a hope.*

*The LORD is good to those who wait
for Him, to the soul who seeks Him.*
—Lamentations 3:25 NKJV

*But those who wait on the LORD shall
renew their strength; they shall mount
up with wings like eagles, they shall
run and not be weary, they shall walk
and not faint.* —Isaiah 40:31 NKJV

*We know that in all things God works for the
good of those who love him, who have been
called according to his purpose.* —Romans 8:28

*"For I know the plans that I have for you,"
declares the LORD, "plans for welfare
and not for calamity to give you a future
and a hope."* —Jeremiah 29:11 NASB

Hope is some
extraordinary
spiritual grace
that God gives
us to control
our fears, not
to oust them.

VINCENT MCNABB

Do not be afraid of
[your enemies];
the LORD *your*
God himself will
fight for you.

DEUTERONOMY 3:22

19

PUT YOUR TRUST IN ME, AND I WILL KEEP YOU SAFE. There is a deep, deep yearning in your heart for safety and security. You can mask these longings with activity for a time, but *only* for a time. These feelings actually serve a very good purpose. Properly used, they can point you to Me and My sufficiency. I am the only One who can really, ultimately keep you safe.

Whenever you start to feel insecure—about *anything*—come to Me. Talk with Me about your fears and concerns; then affirm your trust in Me. Voicing your trust connects you with Me at a deep level. It also pushes back the darkness of deception. The evil one has been deceiving people ever since time began, since the Garden of Eden. Do not listen to his lies. Instead, put your trust in Me, for I am absolute Truth. As you come to know Me—*the Truth*—better and better, I make you increasingly free.

Fear of man will prove to be a snare,
*but whoever trusts in the L*ORD *is*
kept safe. —Proverbs 29:25

*The L*ORD *God said to the woman, "What is*
this you have done?" The woman said, "The
serpent deceived me, and I ate." —Genesis 3:13

Jesus said to [Thomas], "I am the way, the
truth, and the life. No one comes to the Father
except through Me." —John 14:6 NKJV

"And you shall know the truth, and the truth
shall make you free." —John 8:32 NKJV

20

I am Sovereign, and I am Good. These are essential truths about who I am. When you are struggling with the brokenness of this world, it can be a challenge to believe both truths simultaneously. Because I am Sovereign, I am ultimately in control of everything that happens—to you and to others. This knowledge is sometimes hard to swallow, especially in the face of atrocities or catastrophes. Amid such carnage, many people conclude that only a cruel God could be overseeing a world like this.

Let me assure you that I am absolutely Good. I am pure Light, and there is not an iota of darkness in Me. My absolute Goodness in the face of so much evil is totally beyond your understanding. When you are struggling with these mysteries, come to Me. Express yourself freely to Me, trusting that I care and understand. Then, subordinate your finite mind to My infinite intelligence and sovereign ways. Relinquish your demand to understand, and rest in My compassionate Presence. Cling to Me in childlike trust, believing that *My way*—though mysterious— *is perfect.*

He will swallow up death forever. The Sovereign LORD will wipe away the tears from all faces; he will remove the disgrace of his people from all the earth. The LORD has spoken. —Isaiah 25:8

This is the message which we have heard from Him and declare to you, that God is light and in Him is no darkness at all. —1 John 1:5 NKJV

As for God, His way is perfect; the word of the LORD is proven; He is a shield to all who trust in Him. —Psalm 18:30 NKJV

21

CONFESS YOUR SINS TO ME. Do not be afraid to face yourself honestly—in My Presence. In this brilliant Light you can see many things that miss the mark of My perfect standard. Though this is uncomfortable, do not try to run away or shift blame. Instead, agree with Me about these matters, and leave them with Me. Rejoice because I have already paid the penalty—taken the whole punishment—for all your sins. Joyfully receive the forgiveness I bought for you with My own blood.

When I forgive you, I also *cleanse you from all unrighteousness.* I even clothe you in My own perfect righteousness. As you *walk in the Light* with Me, there is a continual cleansing work going on within you. This purifying work of My blood helps you stay close to Me and to others who walk in My Light.

Blessed are those who walk in the Light of My Presence. They rejoice in My Name all day long, exulting in My righteousness.

If we confess our sins, He is faithful and just to forgive us our sins and to cleanse us from all unrighteousness. —1 John 1:9 NKJV

I delight greatly in the LORD; my soul rejoices in my God. For he has clothed me with garments of salvation and arrayed me in a robe of righteousness, as a bridegroom adorns his head like a priest, and as a bride adorns herself with her jewels. —Isaiah 61:10

If we walk in the light, as he is in the light, we have fellowship with one another, and the blood of Jesus, his Son, purifies us from all sin. —1 John 1:7

Blessed are those who have learned to acclaim you, who walk in the light of your presence, O LORD. They rejoice in your name all day long; they exult in your righteousness. —Psalm 89:15–16

22

I GUIDE YOU IN THE WAY OF WISDOM and lead you along straight paths. I know how confused you sometimes feel—and how much you long to find the way forward. You have tried so many different things; you have been so hopeful at times. Yet your hope-filled paths have led to disappointment. I want you to know that I fully understand how hard your journey has been. I also assure you that I can bring good out of every bit of it.

This is *the way of wisdom*: trusting Me no matter what happens in your life. It is through trust that you follow Me along the right path. There are many things that seem random or wrong as you go along your journey. Yet I am able to fit them all into a comprehensive *plan for good*—My Master Plan. So don't be fooled by the way things appear at a given point in time. You are looking at only a very small piece of a massively big picture. From your limited perspective, your journey may be confusing, with puzzling twists and turns. However, from My limitless, big-picture perspective, I am indeed *leading you along straight paths.*

*I guide you in the way of wisdom and lead
you along straight paths. —Proverbs 4:11*

*We are assured and know that [God being a
partner in their labor] all things work together
and are [fitting into a plan] for good to and for
those who love God and are called according to
[His] design and purpose. —Romans 8:28 AMP*

*A man's steps are directed by the Lord.
How then can anyone understand
his own way? —Proverbs 20:24*

23

LET ME FILL YOU WITH MY JOY AND PEACE. They flow into you as you sit quietly in My Presence, trusting Me in the depths of your being. These blessings are essential for nourishing your soul. *The Joy of the Lord is your strength*, so don't neglect this delightful gift. It is for all times and all circumstances, though sometimes you have to search for it. You also need My Peace at all times, and I bestow it on you freely as you trust in Me.

Remember that I am *the God of hope*. The hope I offer is not wishful thinking. It is absolutely certain, even though it refers to things not yet fully realized. It is utterly secure because I Myself obtained it through My finished work on the cross. This hope is the foundation of the Joy and Peace you find in Me. No matter how hard your life may be at this time, you have full assurance that endless delight awaits you in heaven, where I have *prepared a place for you*. As you ponder this glorious truth, you can enjoy hope that *overflows by the Power of the Holy Spirit*.

*May the God of hope fill you with all joy
and peace as you trust in him, so that
you may overflow with hope by the power
of the Holy Spirit.* —Romans 15:13

*Then [Nehemiah] said to [all the people of
Israel], "Go your way, eat the fat, drink the
sweet, and send portions to those for whom
nothing is prepared; for this day is holy to our
Lord. Do not sorrow, for the joy of the LORD
is your strength."* —Nehemiah 8:10 NKJV

*"In My Father's house are many mansions;
if it were not so, I would have told you. I go
to prepare a place for you. And if I go and
prepare a place for you, I will come again
and receive you to Myself; that where I am,
there you may be also."* —John 14:2–3 NKJV

Hope is a golden cord connecting you to heaven. This cord helps you hold your head up high, even when multiple trials are buffeting you. . . . Hope lifts your perspective from your weary feet to the glorious view you can see from the high road. You are reminded that the road we're traveling together is ultimately a highway to heaven.

JESUS CALLING

As it is written:
"No eye has
seen, no ear has
heard, no mind
has conceived
what God has
prepared for those
who love him."

1 Corinthians 2:9

24

WHEN YOU ARE GOING THROUGH A DARK TIME—a hard time—it's easy to project that darkness into the future. The longer you struggle with adverse circumstances, the darker the way before you appears—and the harder it is to imagine yourself walking along bright paths again. The temptation is to just give up and let misery become your companion. So it is crucial at such times to remember that *I* am your constant Companion. Moreover, because I am Sovereign God, I am able to *turn your darkness into Light.*

When you feel on the verge of sinking in despair, turn to Me for help. Cling to My hand, and *walk by faith* through the darkness. Do not focus on the circumstances that are weighing you down. Instead, through eyes of faith, look ahead to brighter times, and praise Me for them. While you worship Me in the midst of darkness, I enable you to see *the first gleam of dawn* on the path before you. Continue walking worshipfully with Me—a walk of faith. As you persevere along this path, the dim light will gradually *shine brighter and brighter till the full light of day.*

The Spirit of the Sovereign LORD is on me, because the LORD has anointed me to preach good news to the poor. He has sent me to bind up the brokenhearted, to proclaim freedom for the captives and release from darkness for the prisoners. —Isaiah 61:1

You are my lamp, O LORD; the LORD turns my darkness into light. —2 Samuel 22:29

We walk by faith, not by sight. —2 Corinthians 5:7 NKJV

The path of the righteous is like the first gleam of dawn, shining ever brighter till the full light of day. —Proverbs 4:18

25

GAZE AT ME; GLANCE AT PROBLEMS—this is the secret of living victoriously. Your tendency is to gaze at problems for prolonged periods of time, glancing at Me for help. This is natural for someone with a fallen mind living in a fallen world. However, I have called you to live *supernaturally*, and I have empowered you to do so. The Holy Spirit, who lives in all My followers, enables you to live beyond yourself—to transcend your natural tendencies.

Ask My Spirit to help you fix your gaze on Me. Invite Him to alert you whenever you get overly focused on problems so you can redirect your attention to Me. This is hard work because it is not only unnatural but also countercultural. Moreover, the evil one and his demons seek to distract you from My Presence. All these influenccs working together put massive pressure on you to pay attention to your problems—or else! So you need the assistance of My Spirit continually. Ask Him to help you deal with difficulties as needed, while reserving the bulk of your attention for Me—your constant Companion.

Let us fix our eyes on Jesus, the author and perfecter of our faith, who for the joy set before him endured the cross, scorning its shame, and sat down at the right hand of the throne of God. —Hebrews 12:2

"I will pray the Father, and He will give you another Helper, that He may abide with you forever—the Spirit of truth, whom the world cannot receive, because it neither sees Him nor knows Him; but you know Him, for He dwells with you and will be in you." —John 14:16–17 NKJV

We fix our eyes not on what is seen, but on what is unseen. For what is seen is temporary, but what is unseen is eternal. —2 Corinthians 4:18

26

TRUST IN ME FOREVER, FOR I AM THE ROCK ETERNAL. It is easy to trust Me for a while—especially when things are going well in your life. But I am calling you to trust in Me *at all times,* no matter what is happening. I understand what a difficult assignment this is, and I know that you will sometimes fail in this venture. But I continue to love you perfectly even when you don't succeed. Let this assurance of My unfailing Love draw you back to Me— back to trusting Me.

Though your trust is imperfect and unsteady, I am *the Rock eternal*—absolutely steady and unchanging. You can rely on Me! When your walk through this world feels wobbly, remember that I am your Rock. I always provide a stable place for you to stand. I can easily bear all your weight, including the weight of your problems. So come to Me when you are feeling *heavy laden* with worries. I invite you to *lean on Me—trusting Me with all your heart and mind.*

*Trust in the L*ord *forever, for the L*ord, *the L*ord, *is the Rock eternal. —Isaiah 26:4*

"Come to Me, all you who labor and are heavy laden, and I will give you rest." —Matthew 11:28 NKJV

Lean on, trust in, and be confident in the Lord with all your heart and mind and do not rely on your own insight or understanding. —Proverbs 3:5 AMP

27

BE JOYFUL IN HOPE. Sometimes the circumstances of your life (and the condition of this world) make it difficult for you to be joyful. When you're searching for Joy, where do you turn? One of the best places to find true Joy is in hope. I want you to know *the hope to which I have called you—the riches of My glorious inheritance.* Since you are a co-heir with Me, this blessing is definitely for you. When present circumstances are weighing you down, grasp on to hope for dear life! It will help you not only to survive but to thrive—to live joyously.

In some ways, hope is like a hot-air balloon. It is very buoyant, so it can lift you up above your troubles. It enables you to soar in the heavens with Me—helping you see things from a heightened, big-picture perspective. To embark on this heavenly journey, you must climb into the basket beneath the balloon—by trusting fully that your hope in Me will not let you down. *There is surely a future hope for you, and your hope will not be cut off.*

Be joyful in hope, patient in affliction, faithful in prayer. —Romans 12:12

[May God] give you the Spirit of wisdom and of revelation in the knowledge of him, having the eyes of your hearts enlightened, that you may know what is the hope to which he has called you, what are the riches of his glorious inheritance in the saints. —Ephesians 1:17–18 ESV

There is surely a future hope for you, and your hope will not be cut off. —Proverbs 23:18

28

THOUGH YOU WALK IN THE MIDST OF TROUBLE, I will revive you. So don't let problems intimidate you. Remember that I, *the Mighty One,* am *in your midst,* and I am greater than all the trouble in the world. *My right hand will save you!* Hold tightly to My hand, and you can walk confidently through your toughest times.

I enable you not only to endure your hardships but also to grow stronger through them. However, because you are on an arduous journey, there will be times when you feel weary and faint. Do not interpret this as a sign of My displeasure with you. It is simply part of living in a fallen, sin-stained world. Remember that you are not alone: I am with you, and *your brothers throughout the world* are experiencing *the same kind of sufferings* as you. Stay in communication with Me as you persevere along this challenging path. My living Presence will revive you—strengthening you and *blessing you with Peace.*

Though I walk in the midst of trouble, You will revive me; You will stretch out Your hand against the wrath of my enemies, and Your right hand will save me. —Psalm 138:7 NKJV

The LORD your God in your midst, the Mighty One, will save; He will rejoice over you with gladness, He will quiet you with His love, He will rejoice over you with singing. —Zephaniah 3:17 NKJV

Resist [your enemy the devil], standing firm in the faith, because you know that your brothers throughout the world are undergoing the same kind of sufferings. —1 Peter 5:9

The LORD gives strength to his people; the LORD blesses his people with peace. —Psalm 29:11

29

YOU ARE IN ME, AND I AM IN YOU. This is a profound mystery. I am the infinite Creator and Sustainer of the entire universe. You are a finite, fallen human being. Yet you and I live not just *with* each other but also *in* each other. You are filled with My *divine Presence*. This is a deeper, fuller union than you can find in any human relationship. Even people who have been married many decades cannot know all the thoughts and feelings of their spouse. But I know *everything* about you—from your deepest thoughts and feelings to the events you will encounter tomorrow. For My children, aloneness is really just an illusion. The whole world is alive with My vibrant Presence!

In Me you live and move and have your being. Every step you take, every word you speak, every breath you breathe—all is done in My watchful, embracing Presence. You are totally immersed in My invisible yet ever-so-real Being! The more aware of Me you are, the more alive and complete you will feel. Your union with Me makes every moment of your life meaningful.

*"On that day you will realize that I am in my Father,
and you are in me, and I am in you."* —John 14:20

*To [His saints] God willed to make known
what are the riches of the glory of this mystery
among the Gentiles: which is Christ in you,
the hope of glory.* —Colossians 1:27 NKJV

*May you be rooted deep in love and founded securely
on love . . . [that you may really come] to know
[practically, through experience for yourselves] the
love of Christ, which far surpasses mere knowledge
[without experience]; that you may be filled [through
all your being] unto all the fullness of God [may
have the richest measure of the divine Presence,
and become a body wholly filled and flooded
with God Himself]!* —Ephesians 3:17, 19 AMP

*"For in [God] we live and move and have
our being." As some of your own poets have
said, "We are his offspring."* —Acts 17:28

30

CAST YOUR BURDEN ON ME, AND I WILL SUSTAIN YOU. No matter what your circumstances may be, I can—and will—carry you through them. Sometimes you are weighed down by a situation that seems too heavy for you. Do not try to cope with this burden alone. Instead, bring it into My Presence and cast it on Me, releasing it into My care and keeping. Although your circumstances may not change right away, you can find real relief through this process.

Casting your burden on Me is a spiritual transaction. You acknowledge that I am in charge of your life and that outcomes are ultimately *My* domain. This lightens your load immensely, relieving you from feeling responsible for things beyond your control.

When you *come to Me weary and burdened*, I have promised that *I will give you rest. Take My yoke upon you*—trusting in *My unfailing Love*—and let Me carry your heavy load. *For My yoke is easy and My burden is light.*

Cast your burden on the LORD, and He shall sustain you; He shall never permit the righteous to be moved. —Psalm 55:22 NKJV

"Come to me, all you who are weary and burdened, and I will give you rest. Take my yoke upon you and learn from me, for I am gentle and humble in heart, and you will find rest for your souls. For my yoke is easy and my burden is light." —Matthew 11:28–30

I trust in your unfailing love; my heart rejoices in your salvation. —Psalm 13:5

Christianity is realistic
because it says that
if there is no truth,
there is also no hope.

Francis A. Schaeffer

Revive me, O Lord, according to Your lovingkindness. The sum of Your word is truth, and every one of Your righteous ordinances is everlasting.

Psalm 119:159–160 NASB

31

COME TO ME WHEN YOU ARE HURTING. Voice your trust in Me, and seek to become aware of My Love all around you. Breathe in the Peace of My Presence: *Peace that transcends understanding.* Take time, take time with Me.

To experience the Joy of My Presence, you need to sit quietly, focusing your thoughts on Me. Say *no* to plans and problems as they try to creep into your mind. Say *yes* to Me—to My Joy and Peace, My unfailing Love.

Living close to Me is all about transcendence. The world is full of trouble, but *I have overcome the world*! I call you to transcend your troubles by looking up to Me. Assert your confidence in Me, saying, "I trust You, Jesus. You are my Hope." Short prayers such as these—voiced almost continuously—will help you live transcendently: *seated with Me in heavenly realms.* I am training you to be an overcomer—unfettered by circumstances.

Do not be anxious about anything, but in everything, by prayer and petition, with thanksgiving, present your requests to God. And the peace of God, which transcends all understanding, will guard your hearts and your minds in Christ Jesus. —Philippians 4:6–7

"These things I have spoken to you, that in Me you may have peace. In the world you will have tribulation; but be of good cheer, I have overcome the world." —John 16:33 NKJV

God raised us up with Christ and seated us with him in the heavenly realms in Christ Jesus. —Ephesians 2:6

32

I ALWAYS LEAD YOU *FORWARD*. When you are going through hard times, you tend to look back longingly at seasons when your life seemed easier, less complicated. You daydream about those simpler times—looking at them through rose-colored lenses. Even your prayers reflect this yearning to go back to earlier, easier circumstances. But this is not My way for you!

Because of the nature of time, there is only one direction to travel, and that is *forward*. Your life on earth is a journey—beginning at birth and ending at the gates of heaven. I am your Guide, and your responsibility is to follow Me wherever I lead. Sometimes I take you to places you would rather not go, but this is My prerogative as your Savior-God. I am also your Shepherd. I always lead you along the best possible path—no matter how painful or confusing it may be. When your path takes you through a dark valley and you are struggling, look to Me for help. Follow Me obediently, trusting Me in the midst of darkness and confusion. I am tenderly present with you each step of your journey. As you stay close to Me, I show you the way forward. Little by little, *I turn your darkness into Light.*

This [Jesus] spoke, signifying by what death [Peter] would glorify God. And when He had spoken this, He said to him, "Follow Me." —John 21:19 NKJV

The LORD is my shepherd, I shall not be in want. . . . Even though I walk through the valley of the shadow of death, I will fear no evil, for you are with me; your rod and your staff, they comfort me. —Psalm 23:1, 4

You, O LORD, keep my lamp burning; my God turns my darkness into light. —Psalm 18:28

33

I WILL FIGHT FOR YOU; YOU NEED ONLY TO BE STILL.
I know how weary you are, My child. You have been
struggling just to keep your head above water, and your
strength is running low. Now is the time for you to stop
striving and let Me fight for you. I know this is not easy
for you to do. You feel as if you must keep struggling in
order to survive, but I am calling you to rest in Me. I
am working on your behalf; so *be still, and know that I
am God.*

Quieting your body is somewhat challenging for you,
but stilling your mind may often seem downright impossible. In your striving to feel secure, you have relied too
heavily on your own thinking. This struggle to be in control has elevated your mind to a position of autonomy. So
you need the intervention of the Holy Spirit. Ask Him to
control your mind more and more—soothing you from
the inside out. Take time to *rest in the shadow of the
Almighty* while I fight for you.

The Lᴏʀᴅ will fight for you; you need only to be still. —Exodus 14:14

Be still, and know that I am God; I will be exalted among the nations, I will be exalted in the earth! —Psalm 46:10 ɴᴋᴊᴠ

The mind of sinful man is death, but the mind controlled by the Spirit is life and peace. —Romans 8:6

He who dwells in the shelter of the Most High will rest in the shadow of the Almighty. —Psalm 91:1

34

CHRISTIAN HOPE IS STRONGLY LINKED to My Presence—which is with you now and throughout eternity. So the more aware you are of My Presence, the more hopeful you will feel. Even though you believe that *I am with you always*, there may be times when you feel distant from Me. This diminishes your hopefulness.

Do not hesitate to ask for My help. For instance, you can simply pray, "Jesus, keep me aware of You." This prayer is so short and simple that you can use it as often as needed. Sometimes you limp through a day feeling empty and alone. But I say to you at such times, *"You do not have because you do not ask."*

Hoping in Me is the most realistic way to live because of who I am. Since I am the Creator and Sustainer of the universe, nothing can thwart My promises. As you marvel at how great, glorious, and trustworthy I am, your praises will fill you with hope—and with rich awareness of My Presence.

Why are you in despair, O my soul? And why have you become disturbed within me? Hope in God, for I shall again praise Him for the help of His presence. —Psalm 42:5 NASB

"Go and make disciples of all nations . . . teaching them to obey everything I have commanded you. And surely I am with you always, to the very end of the age." —Matthew 28:19–20

You lust and do not have. You murder and covet and cannot obtain. You fight and war. Yet you do not have because you do not ask. —James 4:2 NKJV

35

THOUGH I BRING GRIEF, I WILL SHOW COMPASSION. So do not despair when hard times come your way, and do not try to escape them prematurely. Timing is My prerogative! *There is a time for everything, and a season for every activity under heaven.* Grief is a season, and I use it for your good.

Unlike the four seasons of the year, the seasons of your life are not orderly or predictable. When you are grieving, you may feel as if sorrow will accompany you the rest of your days. But remember that I have promised to show compassion. *So great is My unfailing Love* for you!

When you are suffering, search for signs of My merciful Presence. Even during your darkest days, streaks of Light break through the storm clouds—providing hope and comfort. My unfailing Love shines upon you always. Look up to Me and see My Face shining down upon you. I never run out of compassions. *They are new every morning.*

Though [the Lord] brings grief, he will show compassion, so great is his unfailing love. —Lamentations 3:32

There is a time for everything, and a season for every activity under heaven. —Ecclesiastes 3:1

The Lord make His face shine upon you, and be gracious to you. —Numbers 6:25 NKJV

Through the Lord's mercies we are not consumed, because His compassions fail not. They are new every morning; great is Your faithfulness. "The Lord is my portion," says my soul, "therefore I hope in Him!" —Lamentations 3:22–24 NKJV

36

I AM *IN YOUR MIDST*, AND I AM MIGHTY! JUST as the sun is at the center of the solar system, so I am at the center of your entire being—physical, emotional, and spiritual. I, *the Mighty One* who created the universe, live *inside* you! Let this amazing truth reverberate in your mind and soak into your innermost being.

Ponder what it means to have so much Power dwelling inside you. One implication is that you don't need to worry about your lack of strength. In fact, my Power *shows itself most effective in your weakness.*

Remind yourself frequently that I live inside you and I am mighty! Let your awareness of My indwelling Presence drive out discouragement and fill you *with great Joy.* As My Life flows into yours, you are strengthened with divine might.

*The Lord your God in your midst, the
Mighty One, will save; He will rejoice
over you with gladness, He will quiet you
with His love, He will rejoice over you
with singing. —Zephaniah 3:17 NKJV*

*[The Lord] said to me, My grace (My favor and
loving-kindness and mercy) is enough for you
[sufficient against any danger and enables you
to bear the trouble manfully]; for My strength
and power are made perfect (fulfilled and
completed) and show themselves most effective
in [your] weakness. Therefore, I will all the more
gladly glory in my weaknesses and infirmities,
that the strength and power of Christ (the
Messiah) may rest (yes, may pitch a tent over
and dwell) upon me! —2 Corinthians 12:9 AMP*

*To him who is able to keep you from falling
and to present you before his glorious presence
without fault and with great joy. —Jude 24*

No other religion, no other, promises new bodies, hearts, and minds. Only in the gospel of Christ do hurting people find such incredible hope.

Joni Eareckson Tada

*"God will wipe
away every tear
from their eyes;
there shall be no
more death, nor
sorrow, nor crying.
There shall be no
more pain, for
the former things
have passed away."
Then He who sat
on the throne said,
"Behold, I make
all things new."*

Revelation 21:4–5 nkjv

37

I CROWN YOU WITH LOVINGKINDNESS and tender mercies. You need vast quantities of these blessings, and I delight in providing them for you. Your job is to open your heart fully to Me, acknowledging—to yourself and to Me—how needy you are. Many people are afraid to face their neediness because they doubt that anyone could ever provide all that they lack. Humanly speaking, this is true. But I have infinite reservoirs of blessings for My children. Moreover, My lovingkindness is an eternal gift, for *I have loved you with an everlasting Love.* I am committed to you!

All of My children need mercy—compassionate treatment—and you are no exception. I offer you multiple mercies, and I do this tenderly. So come to Me when you are feeling weak and vulnerable. *Pour out your heart to Me,* and rest in My Presence. Remember that you are redeemed royalty, purchased with My own blood. Hold still—with dignity and confidence—while I *crown you with lovingkindness and tender mercies.*

Bless the LORD, O my soul; and all that is within me, bless His holy name! Bless the LORD, O my soul, and forget not all His benefits: who forgives all your iniquities, who heals all your diseases, who redeems your life from destruction, who crowns you with lovingkindness and tender mercies. —Psalm 103:1–4 NKJV

The LORD has appeared of old to me, saying: "Yes, I have loved you with an everlasting love; therefore with lovingkindness I have drawn you." —Jeremiah 31:3 NKJV

Trust in him at all times, O people; pour out your hearts to him, for God is our refuge. —Psalm 62:8

38

YOU BELONG TO ME. I HAVE CHOSEN YOU and *called you out of darkness into My marvelous Light.* The fact that you belong to Me—now and forever—provides a firm foundation for your life. This connection with Me can protect you from feeling cut off or adrift in your ever-changing world. Many people attach themselves to hurtful people or harmful things because they yearn to escape their aloneness. But you are *never* alone, for you are Mine. I chose you *before the creation of the world,* and you are a permanent member of My royal family.

You used to walk in spiritual darkness before you trusted Me as Savior. I personally brought you out of that darkness into My Light—so that you might *proclaim My praises.* This is a delightful privilege and responsibility. I have entrusted you with the task of telling others about My awesome qualities. To carry out this assignment effectively, you need to delve into the riches of who I am by studying My Word. You also need to *delight yourself in Me.* Then the Joy of My Presence will shine from your face as you tell others about Me.

You are a chosen generation, a royal priesthood, a holy nation, His own special people, that you may proclaim the praises of Him who called you out of darkness into His marvelous light. —1 Peter 2:9 NKJV

Praise be to the God and Father of our Lord Jesus Christ, who has blessed us in the heavenly realms with every spiritual blessing in Christ. For he chose us in him before the creation of the world to be holy and blameless in his sight. —Ephesians 1:3–4

Delight yourself in the LORD and he will give you the desires of your heart. —Psalm 37:4

39

BE STRONG AND COURAGEOUS. *Do not be discouraged, for I will be with you wherever you go.* You can choose to be strong and courageous even when you are feeling very weak. However, the weaker you feel, the more effort it takes to *choose* to be strong. It all depends on where you look. If you gaze at yourself and your problems, your courage will melt away. The choice to be bold rests on your confidence that I am *with* you and *for* you. Through eyes of faith, see Me on the path before you, beckoning you on, one step at a time. Looking to Me consistently will increase your strength and valor.

When everything seems to be going wrong, refuse to get discouraged. Remember that I am a God of surprises: I am not limited by the way things are or by the paltry possibilities you can see. I am infinitely creative and powerful. *With Me all things are possible!* The longer you wait for your prayers to be answered, the closer you are to a breakthrough. Meanwhile, waiting for Me—aware of My loving Presence—is a blessed way to live. *I am good to those who wait for Me.*

Have I not commanded you? Be strong and courageous. Do not be terrified; do not be discouraged, for the LORD your God will be with you wherever you go. —Joshua 1:9

Jesus looked at them and said to them, "With men this is impossible, but with God all things are possible." —Matthew 19:26 NKJV

The LORD is good to those who wait for Him, to the soul who seeks Him. It is good that one should hope and wait quietly for the salvation of the LORD. —Lamentations 3:25–26 NKJV

40

HUMBLE YOURSELF UNDER MY MIGHTY HAND. You are well aware of My powerful hand working in your life experiences. Sometimes you feel weighed down by My Sovereign will—trapped by circumstances you cannot change. The temptation at such times is to grow impatient with Me and My ways. But this will only frustrate you further, and your negative feelings will pull you down. Your impatience will also alienate you from Me.

When you are feeling weighed down by your circumstances, change your perspective by looking up to Me. Muster the courage to say, "Lord, I humble myself under Your mighty hand." Submit to Me and My ways in your life, even though you long to break free. This protects you from fighting against Me—the Creator and Sustainer of the universe. Instead of engaging in this battle you cannot win, use your energy to cope with the situation and learn from it. Trust that I will *lift you up*—relieve your suffering—in My perfect, wisely appointed time.

*Humble yourselves, therefore, under
God's mighty hand, that he may lift
you up in due time.* —1 Peter 5:6

*He has shown you, O man, what is good;
and what does the LORD require of you
but to do justly, to love mercy, and to walk
humbly with your God?* —Micah 6:8 NKJV

*[God] gives more grace. Therefore He says:
"God resists the proud, but gives grace
to the humble." . . . Humble yourselves
in the sight of the Lord, and He will
lift you up.* —James 4:6, 10 NKJV

41

YOUR LIFE CAN BE GOOD even when many things are not going as you would like. You yearn to feel more in control of your life, but this is not My way for you. I want you to learn to relax more in My sovereignty, receiving each day as a good gift from Me—no matter what it contains. Remember that you are not responsible for things beyond your control. Accept the limitations of being a finite person and keep turning toward Me. *Cease striving and know that I am God.* Awareness of My Face shining upon you can instill Joy into the most difficult day.

Let Me guide you step by step through this day. Because you are My follower, you live in the midst of fierce spiritual battles. Even your most routine day will have some minor spiritual skirmishes. So *be on the alert* as you follow Me along your life-path. Use your *shield of faith to extinguish all the flaming arrows of the evil one.* Recognize and reject the demonic lies that assault you day and night. Rest in the truth of who you really are: My beloved child in whom I delight.

Cease striving and know that I am God; I will be exalted among the nations, I will be exalted in the earth. —Psalm 46:10 NASB

The LORD make His face shine upon you, and be gracious to you. —Numbers 6:25 NKJV

Be of sober spirit, be on the alert. Your adversary, the devil, prowls around like a roaring lion, seeking someone to devour. —1 Peter 5:8 NASB

Take up the shield of faith, with which you can extinguish all the flaming arrows of the evil one. —Ephesians 6:16

42

WHEN YOU ARE FEELING OVERWHELMED by your circumstances, take time to listen to Me. Hear Me saying, *"Take courage! It is I. Don't be afraid."*

Listening to Me when you're feeling stressed requires discipline and trust. Your racing thoughts make it hard to hear My *gentle whisper.* Ask the Holy Spirit to calm your mind so that you can hear My voice. Remember that I—the *Prince of Peace*—am with you at all times.

I am not only with you; I am also in your circumstances. Moreover, I am in control of everything that happens to you. Although I am never the author of evil, I am fully able to use bad things for good. This does not remove your suffering, but it *does* redeem it—infusing it with meaning. So if you are in a storm of difficulties, I say to you, *"Take courage. It is I."* Search for signs of My abiding Presence in your current situation. *You will seek Me and find Me when you search for Me with all your heart.*

Jesus immediately said to them: "Take courage! It is I. Don't be afraid." —Matthew 14:27

After the earthquake came a fire, but the Lord was not in the fire. And after the fire came a gentle whisper. —1 Kings 19:12

For unto us a Child is born, unto us a Son is given; and the government will be upon His shoulder. And His name will be called Wonderful, Counselor, Mighty God, Everlasting Father, Prince of Peace. —Isaiah 9:6 NKJV

You will seek Me and find Me, when you search for Me with all your heart. —Jeremiah 29:13 NKJV

Hope is faith
holding out its
hand in the dark.

GEORGE ILES

*We who have
fled to him for
refuge can have
great confidence
as we hold to the
hope that lies
before us. This
hope is a strong
and trustworthy
anchor for our
souls. It leads
us through the
curtain into God's
inner sanctuary.*

HEBREWS 6:18–19 NLT

43

BEWARE OF FEELING ENTITLED to My good gifts. Receive blessings from Me thankfully, yet be willing to release them back to Me—without growing resentful.

When you have lost something precious (your job, your house, your health, a loved one), you may think it is irrational to be joyful. But this is a worldly way of thinking. Major losses are very painful, and they do need to be grieved. Nonetheless, with time and effort you can learn to focus on the good things that remain—and find Joy in the One who *will never leave you.*

Remember that it is possible to be *sorrowful, yet always rejoicing.* The apostle Paul learned the secret of being joyful in all situations through his experiences of multiple hardships. The Holy Spirit empowered Paul to find Joy in the midst of adversity, and He can do the same for you. You must be willing, though, to let go of anything I take from you—no matter how painful the loss. Then direct your attention fully to Me, trusting that I will never let go of *you.*

*Be strong and courageous. Do not be afraid
or terrified because of them, for the* LORD
*your God goes with you; he will never leave
you nor forsake you.* —Deuteronomy 31:6

*In all things we commend ourselves as
ministers of God . . . as sorrowful, yet always
rejoicing; as poor, yet making many rich;
as having nothing, and yet possessing all
things.* —2 Corinthians 6:4, 10 NKJV

*I am always with you; you hold me by
my right hand. You guide me with your
counsel, and afterward you will take
me into glory.* —Psalm 73:23–24

44

BELOVED, FIND REST IN ME ALONE. *Your hope comes from Me.*

Rest and hope make a wonderful combination, and you can find plenty of both in Me. Some people search for the best bed or pillow—or even sleeping pill—in their quest for deep sleep, but only *I* can provide what you really need. When you rest trustingly in My Presence, I not only refresh you—I fill you with hope.

Hope can make the difference between life and death. Prisoners of war who stop hoping are much less likely to survive. The same is true of people who are battling life-threatening illnesses. So it is important to nurture well your precious hope. It is also vital to place your hope ultimately in *Me.* Circumstances change all the time, but I am *the same yesterday, today, and forever.* Moreover, I love you with perfect, life-giving Love. *My unfailing Love rests upon you as you put your hope in Me.*

Find rest, O my soul, in God alone; my hope comes from him. He alone is my rock and my salvation; he is my fortress, I will not be shaken. —Psalm 62:5–6

About Benjamin [Moses] said: "Let the beloved of the L<small>ORD</small> rest secure in him, for he shields him all day long, and the one the L<small>ORD</small> loves rests between his shoulders." —Deuteronomy 33:12

Jesus Christ is the same yesterday, today, and forever. —Hebrews 13:8 <small>NKJV</small>

May your unfailing love rest upon us, O L<small>ORD</small>, even as we put our hope in you. —Psalm 33:22

45

I AM WATCHING OVER YOU CONTINUALLY. No matter what you are experiencing or how alone you feel, trust that I am with you—well aware of your circumstances. When you are in the throes of adversity, it is easy to feel abandoned. So it is crucial at such times to tell yourself the truth: *Nothing* can separate you from My loving Presence. When this truth has sunk deeply into your mind and heart, you are ready to commune with Me. You will find Me tenderly present with you as I enter into your suffering. The intimacy you share with Me is enhanced by adversity when you invite Me into your experience without bitterness or resentment.

To enjoy these intimate moments with Me, you must trust Me—refusing to *rely on your own understanding*. Trusting Me involves consciously leaning on Me for support, just as leaning on a massive rock helps you keep standing when you are weary. I am indeed *the Rock of your refuge*. Rejoice in the One who supports you so strongly and loves you so tenderly.

I am convinced that neither death nor life, neither angels nor demons, neither the present nor the future, nor any powers, neither height nor depth, nor anything else in all creation, will be able to separate us from the love of God that is in Christ Jesus our Lord. —Romans 8:38–39

Lean on, trust in, and be confident in the Lord with all your heart and mind and do not rely on your own insight or understanding. —Proverbs 3:5 AMP

The Lord has been my defense, and my God the rock of my refuge. —Psalm 94:22 NKJV

46

LET MY PEACE RULE IN YOUR HEART—and be thankful. I have called you to a life of Peace and thankfulness. These two are closely related. The more grateful you are, the better able you are to receive My Peace. Conversely, the more peaceful you are, the easier it is to be grateful. Your calmness helps you to think clearly and to recognize the many blessings I shower upon you. This calm thankfulness is independent of circumstances; it flows out of your confidence that I always do what is best—even when you cannot understand My ways.

My Peace can function as an umpire in your heart, settling the questions and doubts that rise up in your thoughts. Whenever you start to feel anxious, use those feelings as a reminder to communicate with Me. Talk with Me about whatever is disturbing you. Bring Me all your requests *with thanksgiving.* Because you are Mine—intimately united with Me—I personally *guard your heart and mind* with My Peace. Remember that this is supernatural Peace, *which surpasses all understanding.*

Let the peace of Christ rule in your hearts, since as members of one body you were called to peace. And be thankful. —Colossians 3:15

As for God, His way is perfect; the word of the L<small>ORD</small> is proven; He is a shield to all who trust in Him. —Psalm 18:30 <small>NKJV</small>

Be anxious for nothing, but in everything by prayer and supplication, with thanksgiving, let your requests be made known to God; and the peace of God, which surpasses all understanding, will guard your hearts and minds through Christ Jesus. —Philippians 4:6–7 <small>NKJV</small>

47

WHENEVER YOU LOOK FOR ME, YOU WILL FIND ME. My promise to be *with you always* ensures that you never have to face anything alone. This promise is for everyone who has trusted Me as Savior. However, to reap the benefits of this amazing blessing, you must look for Me in the midst of your moments. This sounds like an easy thing to do, but it goes against the grain of the world, the flesh, and the devil.

The evil one uses three *D*s to keep you from finding Me: distractions, deception, and discouragement. The world abounds with things to distract you from Me, so don't be upset when you realize your mind has wandered. Just return to Me with a smile, and whisper My Name in loving contentment. Deception is one of Satan's favorite tactics, from the time of Adam and Eve onward. The best defense against the devil's deceptions is to study and absorb My Word. Discouragement knocks at the door of every human heart at times, but you can refuse to let it in. As you resist these tricky tactics and look for Me, *you will find Me.*

*[Azariah] went out to meet King Asa as he
was returning from battle. "Listen to me, Asa!
Listen, armies of Judah and Benjamin!" he
shouted. "The Lord will stay with you as long
as you stay with him! Whenever you look for
him, you will find him. But if you forsake him,
he will forsake you." —2 Chronicles 15:2 TLB*

*"Go and make disciples of all nations . . .
teaching them to obey everything I
have commanded you. And surely I
am with you always, to the very end
of the age." —Matthew 28:19–20*

*And the LORD God said to the woman,
"What is this you have done?" The
woman said, "The serpent deceived
me, and I ate." —Genesis 3:13 NKJV*

48

HOPE IS *AN ANCHOR FOR YOUR SOUL—firm and secure.* A ship in turbulent waters needs to drop anchor in a safe place. In stormy weather, a large ship may be unable to enter the safety of a harbor because of the wild waves buffeting the boat. So a smaller boat may be used to carry the ship's anchor through the breakers into the harbor. When the anchor is dropped there, the ship is secured—even though it is still in rough waters.

This is a picture of how hope keeps your soul—the eternal part of you—safe and secure in the midst of life's storms. To be effective, your hope must be solidly in Me, the Savior-God who died to pay the penalty for your sins. After I was crucified, My miraculous resurrection empowered Me to be your *living Hope.* In fact, I am more abundantly alive than you can begin to imagine. When your hope is connected to Me, you share in My vibrant, eternal Life. Someday you will have a glorified body like Mine! Meanwhile, be assured that your hope-anchor keeps you secure even in life's fiercest storms.

We [who are holding on to the hope of God's salvation promises] have this hope as an anchor for the soul, firm and secure. It enters the inner sanctuary behind the curtain, where Jesus, who went before us, has entered on our behalf. He has become a high priest forever, in the order of Melchizedek. —Hebrews 6:19–20

Praise be to the God and Father of our Lord Jesus Christ! In his great mercy he has given us new birth into a living hope through the resurrection of Jesus Christ from the dead. —1 Peter 1:3

Let us hold fast the confession of our hope without wavering, for He who promised is faithful. —Hebrews 10:23 NKJV

Even when our
situation appears
to be impossible,
our work is to
"hope in God."
Our hope will
not be in vain,
and in the Lord's
own timing,
help will come.

GEORGE MUELLER

Why are you in despair, O my soul? And why have you become disturbed within me? Hope in God, for I shall again praise Him for the help of His presence.

PSALM 42:5 NASB

49

I CAME INTO YOUR LIFE TO *MAKE YOU FREE.* The closer you live to Me, the freer you can be. By spending time alone with Me, your awareness of My abiding Presence grows deeper and stronger. There is *healing in My wings*—in the intimacy of nearness to Me. My healing Presence binds up wounds from your past so that they stop bleeding. The salve of My Spirit enhances the healing process. In My holy Light you can see things from a new perspective—freeing you from old, unhelpful ways of thinking. As you lay down baggage from your past, you grow increasingly free.

I make you free through the truth—about who I am and what I have done for you. I also help you face the truth about yourself and the people in your life. If you're involved in hurtful relationships, I will help you change them or break free. If you are trapped in addictions, I will help you take the first step toward freedom—honest confession of the truth. In every situation, *the truth will set you free.*

"You shall know the truth, and the truth shall make you free." —John 8:32 NKJV

How great is your goodness, which you have stored up for those who fear you, which you bestow in the sight of men on those who take refuge in you. In the shelter of your presence you hide them from the intrigues of men; in your dwelling you keep them safe from accusing tongues. —Psalm 31:19–20

But for you who revere my name, the sun of righteousness will rise with healing in its wings. And you will go out and leap like calves released. —Malachi 4:2

There is therefore now no condemnation for those who are in Christ Jesus. For the law of the Spirit of life has set you free in Christ Jesus from the law of sin and death. —Romans 8:1–2 ESV

115

50

A CHEERFUL HEART IS GOOD MEDICINE. You have every reason to be cheerful because *I have overcome the world. I have conquered it and deprived it of power to harm you* through My victory on the cross. Moreover, nothing you will ever encounter along your life-path *will be able to separate you from My Love.* As you ponder these glorious truths about all I have done for you, let *good cheer* fill your heart and radiate from your face.

A joyful heart will improve your health—spiritually, emotionally, and physically. So fill your mind with thankful thoughts till your heart overflows with Joy. Take time to praise Me for all that I am—the One from whom all blessings flow. Let Me fill you with My Light and Life, for I designed you to be full of heavenly contents. As these divine nutrients soak into the depths of your being, they strengthen you and enhance your health. *Be of good cheer!*

A cheerful heart is good medicine,
but a crushed spirit dries up the
bones. —Proverbs 17:22

"I have told you these things, so that in Me
you may have [perfect] peace and confidence.
In the world you have tribulation and trials
and distress and frustration; but be of good
cheer [take courage; be confident, certain,
undaunted]! For I have overcome the world.
[I have deprived it of power to harm you and
have conquered it for you.]" —John 16:33 AMP

Neither height nor depth, nor anything
else in all creation, will be able to separate
us from the love of God that is in Christ
Jesus our Lord. —Romans 8:39

51

I am Good and My Love endures forever. So give thanks to Me and praise My Name. The fact that I am good is vitally important for your well-being. If there were even a speck of badness in Me, you would be in trouble. My absolute Goodness guarantees that I always do what is best. You must accept this as a statement of faith, though, because you live on a deeply fallen planet. So it is essential for you to *walk by faith, not by sight,* as you journey through the wilderness of this world.

One of the best ways to find strength for your journey is to give Me thanks and praise. Thanksgiving and praise lift your perspective from your worries and woes to the glorious Treasure you have in Me. Thankfulness puts you in proper alignment with Me—your Creator and Savior. Praise enhances your intimacy with Me because I *inhabit the praises* of My people. The more you praise Me, the closer to Me you will grow. While you are worshiping, remember that *My Love endures forever*!

Enter his gates with thanksgiving and his courts with praise; give thanks to him and praise his name. For the LORD *is good and his love endures forever; his faithfulness continues through all generations.* —Psalm 100:4–5

For we walk by faith, not by sight.
—2 Corinthians 5:7 NKJV

Thou art holy, O thou that inhabitest the praises of Israel. —Psalm 22:3 KJV

Give thanks to the LORD, *for he is good, for his steadfast love endures forever. Give thanks to the God of gods, for his steadfast love endures forever. Give thanks to the Lord of lords, for his steadfast love endures forever.* —Psalm 136:1–3 ESV

52

LET HIM WHO GLORIES GLORY IN THIS, that he understands and knows Me. This world you inhabit is increasingly complex and confusing. You have more information at your fingertips than you could process in a lifetime. There are so many demands on you—from the world, the church, other people, yourself. As a result, it's easy to feel lost and perplexed. To find Peace in this chaotic clutter, you need to set priorities according to My will. It is crucial to make your relationship with Me the top priority—nurturing and strengthening your connection with Me.

Nothing is as important as understanding Me: knowing and loving Me as I truly am. This requires focused time with Me as well as ongoing communication with Me throughout your day. The clearest, most trustworthy teaching about Me is in the Bible. The beauty of nature also proclaims Me and reveals My Glory.

Making Me your highest priority gives focus to your thinking. Other priorities fall into their proper place when I am first and foremost in your life.

"Let him who glories glory in this, that he understands and knows Me, that I am the LORD, exercising lovingkindness, judgment, and righteousness in the earth. For in these I delight," says the LORD. —Jeremiah 9:24 NKJV

The heavens declare the glory of God; the skies proclaim the work of his hands. Day after day they pour forth speech; night after night they display knowledge. —Psalm 19:1–2

Jesus replied: "'Love the Lord your God with all your heart and with all your soul and with all your mind.' This is the first and greatest commandment." —Matthew 22:37–38

53

Come close to Me, and rest in My Presence. I am all around you, closer than the very air you breathe. Trust Me with each breath you take.

Your need for Me is as constant as your need for oxygen. So don't neglect the discipline of practicing My Presence. Because your mind is easily distracted, you must keep coming back to Me again and again. Do not be discouraged by your tendency to wander off in tangents from your true Center in Me. Simply keep making the needed adjustments to return to Me. Make these little corrections joyfully—trusting in *My unfailing Love.*

Use My Name, "Jesus," to reconnect with Me. Whisper it, sing it, shout it—remembering what it means: "The Lord saves." Embellish My Name with words of love and trust. Let your heart overflow with gratitude as you ponder all I am to you, all I have done for you. These practices draw you close to Me and help you rest in My Presence.

Find rest, O my soul, in God alone; my hope comes from him. He alone is my rock and my salvation; he is my fortress, I will not be shaken. —Psalm 62:5–6

I am like an olive tree flourishing in the house of God; I trust in God's unfailing love for ever and ever. —Psalm 52:8

She will bring forth a Son, and you shall call His name Jesus, for He will save His people from their sins. —Matthew 1:21 NKJV

54

REJOICE AND EXULT IN HOPE. Raise a shout of Joy! You have good reason to be joyful, because you're on your way to heaven. I have paid the penalty for your sins and clothed you in My own righteousness. *This* is the basis of hope—for you, for all who truly know Me as Savior. No matter what is going on in your life at this time, your hope in Me is secure. No one will be able to *snatch you out of My hand.* In Me you have absolute, eternal security!

Be constant in prayer—at all times, but especially when you are struggling. During trials, you need close communication with Me more than ever. However, your ability to concentrate may be hampered by stress and fatigue. So make full use of the amazing source of strength within you—My Spirit. Ask the Holy Spirit to *control your mind*: to think through you and pray through you. Your prayers need not be pretty or proper. Just let them flow out of your current situation. As you stay in communication with Me, I help you to *be stead-fast and patient in suffering.*

Rejoice and exult in hope; be steadfast and patient in suffering and tribulation; be constant in prayer. —Romans 12:12 AMP

For the grace of God that brings salvation has appeared to all men. . . . while we wait for the blessed hope—the glorious appearing of our great God and Savior, Jesus Christ. —Titus 2:11, 13

"I give [My followers] eternal life, and they shall never perish; neither shall anyone snatch them out of My hand." —John 10:28 NKJV

The mind of sinful man is death, but the mind controlled by the Spirit is life and peace. —Romans 8:6

Hope is the power
of being cheerful in
circumstances we
know to be desperate.

G. K. CHESTERTON

*Hope in the
LORD; for with
the LORD there is
mercy, and with
Him is abundant
redemption.*

PSALM 130:7 NKJV

55

I WANT YOU TO *LEARN THE SECRET of being content in any and every situation.* Contentment-training is a challenging process; it is learned through enduring a wide range of difficulties. You thought you were fairly advanced in this training, but then the circumstances in your life got harder. On some days you are able to cope well with your hardships. On other days you just want *out*! I am here to help you with your "other days."

Begin by acknowledging how frustrated and upset you are feeling. *Pour out your heart to Me!* Simply releasing your pent-up feelings does you a world of good. Knowing that I hear and understand encourages you even more. Ask Me also to increase your awareness of My Presence with you. Continue talking to Me and listening in the depths of your spirit for My response. Cling to helpful scriptures; bathe your mind and heart in them. Finally, sing praises to Me. This will lift your spirits like nothing else. *It is good to sing praises to My Name; to declare My lovingkindness in the morning, and My faithfulness every night.*

I know what it is to be in need, and I know what it is to have plenty. I have learned the secret of being content in any and every situation, whether well fed or hungry, whether living in plenty or in want. —Philippians 4:12

Trust in him at all times, O people; pour out your hearts to him, for God is our refuge. —Psalm 62:8

It is good to give thanks to the LORD, and to sing praises to Your name, O Most High; to declare Your lovingkindness in the morning, and Your faithfulness every night. —Psalm 92:1–2 NKJV

56

I AM TRAINING YOU in the discipline of perseverance. You are on a long uphill journey, and sometimes it seems endless to you. Looking back, you can see some times of ease and refreshment. Looking ahead, however, you see only a continuing ascent. The top of the mountain you are climbing is nowhere in sight. I know how hard it is for you to keep going day after day. So I say to you, *"Do not become weary and discouraged in your soul."*

You live in a culture dedicated to entertainment and pleasure-seeking. In such a climate, a life of struggle feels alien. If you are not careful, you will succumb to self-pity, a sinful snare. To avoid falling into this trap, remember that I am Sovereign and I am lovingly present with you. Your ongoing struggle is *not* a mistake or a punishment. Try to view it, instead, as a rich opportunity: Your uphill journey keeps you aware of your neediness, so you look to Me for help. The difficulties in your life make your heavenly home more precious and real to you. Even now, as you trustingly whisper My Name, I embrace you in *everlasting Love.*

Consider Him who endured such hostility from sinners against Himself, lest you become weary and discouraged in your souls. —Hebrews 12:3 NKJV

"The Spirit of the Lord GOD is upon Me, because the LORD has anointed Me to preach good tidings to the poor; He has sent Me to heal the brokenhearted, to proclaim liberty to the captives, and the opening of the prison to those who are bound." —Isaiah 61:1 NKJV

Our citizenship is in heaven. And we eagerly await a Savior from there, the Lord Jesus Christ, who by the power that enables him to bring everything under his control, will transform our lowly bodies so that they will be like his glorious body. —Philippians 3:20–21

The LORD appeared to us in the past, saying: "I have loved you with an everlasting love; I have drawn you with loving-kindness." —Jeremiah 31:3

57

In quietness and confidence shall be your strength. When you're in a tough situation, your mind tends to go into overdrive. You mentally rehearse possible solutions at breakneck speed. Your brain becomes a flurry of activity! You scrutinize your own abilities and those of people you might call upon for help. If you find no immediate solution to your problem, you start to feel anxious. When you find this happening, return to Me and rest *in quietness*. Take time to seek My Face and My will rather than rushing ahead without clear direction.

I want you to have confidence in Me and My ways—patiently trusting in Me even when you can't see the way forward. Whereas anxious striving drains you of energy, quiet confidence will give you strength. You can trust that I will not forsake you in your time of need. Keep communicating with Me about your situation, and be willing to wait—without pushing for immediate resolution. *Those who wait for the Lord will gain new strength.*

*Thus says the Lord G*OD*, the Holy One of Israel: "In returning and rest you shall be saved; in quietness and confidence shall be your strength." —Isaiah 30:15* NKJV

*Be strong and courageous. Do not be afraid or terrified because of them, for the L*ORD *your God goes with you; he will never leave you nor forsake you. —Deuteronomy 31:6*

*Those who wait for the L*ORD *will gain new strength; they will mount up with wings like eagles, they will run and not get tired, they will walk and not become weary. —Isaiah 40:31* NASB

133

58

PUT YOUR HOPE IN MY UNFAILING LOVE. You live in a world where failure abounds—in governments and businesses, schools and churches, friends, family, and you. Instantaneous worldwide communication makes the failures all the more evident, all the more heart-wrenching. So the idea of *unfailing Love* is radical; there is no adequate model for it in this world. Clearly, such Love can be found only in Me—in the very essence of who I am.

Even the most devoted parent, friend, or lover will let you down sometimes, but I am the eternal Lover who will never fail you. This is possible because I am infinite, perfect God. Yet I became a Man—with human understanding and empathy. In fact, *My compassions never fail.* So find hope in Me and in My amazing provision for believers—*salvation and righteousness that will never fail.* This hope strengthens you and pleases Me. *I delight in those who put their hope in My unfailing Love.*

*The L*ORD *delights in those who fear him, who put their hope in his unfailing love. —Psalm 147:11*

*Because of the L*ORD'*s great love we are not consumed, for his compassions never fail. —Lamentations 3:22*

We have known and believed the love that God has for us. God is love, and he who abides in love abides in God, and God in him. —1 John 4:16 NKJV

Lift up your eyes to the heavens, look at the earth beneath; the heavens will vanish like smoke, the earth will wear out like a garment and its inhabitants die like flies. But my salvation will last forever, my righteousness will never fail. —Isaiah 51:6

59

I AM *LORD GOD ALMIGHTY,* and I am *holy, holy, holy.*
This threefold repetition of My holiness emphasizes My
utter separateness from sin. I want you to enjoy the wonder of My loving Presence with you always, but do not lose
sight of My holiness. Your awareness that I am holy God
can bless and protect you. It highlights how very privi-
leged you are to know Me as Savior and Friend. Also, it
protects you from being presumptuous or relating to Me
carelessly. Sometimes your communication with Me *will*
be improper, but remembering My holiness can help you
repent quickly.

Even though King David committed some terrible
sins, he was *a man after My own heart* who was very
teachable. When Nathan the prophet rebuked David for
having committed adultery and murder, he repented
immediately, saying, *"I have sinned against the Lord."* So
do not despair when you realize you have sinned. Instead,
turn quickly from the offensive way and turn back toward
Me. I will receive you warmly—with *no condemnation.*

The four living creatures, each having six wings, were full of eyes around and within. And they do not rest day or night, saying: "Holy, holy, holy, Lord God Almighty, who was and is and is to come!" —Revelation 4:8 NKJV

After removing Saul, [God] made David their king. He testified concerning him: "I have found David son of Jesse a man after my own heart; he will do everything I want him to do." —Acts 13:22

So David said to Nathan, "I have sinned against the LORD.*" And Nathan said to David, "The* LORD *also has put away your sin; you shall not die." —2 Samuel 12:13* NKJV

There is now no condemnation for those who are in Christ Jesus. —Romans 8:1

60

MAKE ME YOUR DEFAULT FOCUS. Try to become conscious of what you think about when your mind is at rest. Many people's minds gravitate toward worries, work, plans, food, pleasure seeking. Some of these thoughts are useful, while others are not. Most people are not very aware of their thoughts during their "down times," but I am quite aware of them. I want you to train your mind to turn toward Me more and more. Think about who I am—Creator, Savior, King of kings. Ponder also My amazing, unending Love for you.

Training your mind to make Me your default Focus is not easy. Ask the Holy Spirit to help you in this challenging endeavor, and He will. However, you must be prepared to cooperate with Him. You need to spend some time in quietness—away from the television, the radio, and other distracting noise. Communicate with Me frequently throughout the day. Using a short prayer such as, "Jesus, draw me close to You," can help you return your focus to Me time after time. Also, it is vital to saturate your mind with Scripture, which is all about Me. As you practice these disciplines, you will gradually *be transformed by the renewing of your mind.*

When I consider your heavens, the work of your fingers, the moon and the stars, which you have set in place, what is man that you are mindful of him, the son of man that you care for him? —Psalm 8:3–4

Your word I have hidden in my heart, that I might not sin against You. —Psalm 119:11 NKJV

Do not conform any longer to the pattern of this world, but be transformed by the renewing of your mind. Then you will be able to test and approve what God's will is—his good, pleasing and perfect will. —Romans 12:2

I am your risen,
living Savior!
Through My
resurrection *you
have been born
again to an
ever-living hope.*

JESUS LIVES

Listen, I tell you
a mystery: We
will not all sleep,
but we will all
be changed—in
a flash, in the
twinkling of an eye,
at the last trumpet.
For the trumpet
will sound, the
dead will be raised
imperishable, and
we will be changed.

1 Corinthians 15:51–52

61

I AM THE GOD OF LOVE AND PEACE. Let the splendor of this glorious truth sink into the depths of your heart, mind, and spirit. The One who is always with you is the God of Love and Peace! When you feel a need for more Love, come to Me and let Me lavish it upon you. Whenever you are feeling anxious or afraid, come into My peaceful Presence—and relax in *the everlasting arms* awaiting you.

I want your character to reflect Me more and more. So endeavor to be loving and peaceful in your relationships with other people. When someone irritates or upsets you, try to see traces of Me in that person. Remember that I created everyone *in My own image.* The most effective way to love people is to allow My Love to flow through you to them. My Spirit lives inside you, and you can ask Him to love others through you. To live peacefully, you need to forgive people quickly—including yourself. Make every effort to live close to Me, *the God of Love and Peace.*

Be of good comfort, be of one mind, live in peace; and the God of love and peace will be with you. —2 Corinthians 13:11 NKJV

The eternal God is your refuge, and underneath are the everlasting arms. He will drive out your enemy before you, saying, "Destroy him!" —Deuteronomy 33:27

God created man in His own image; in the image of God He created him; male and female He created them. —Genesis 1:27 NKJV

62

BE OF GOOD COURAGE, *and I will strengthen your heart.* I want My children to be brave—not cowardly. In fact, the Bible contains warnings of dire consequences for *"the cowardly, the unbelieving, the vile, the murderers."*

When you are going through very tough times and there is no relief in sight, you usually start looking for a way out. These escapist longings stem from self-pity and a sense of entitlement: You think you deserve better conditions than your current situation. But when you think this way, you are ignoring My sovereignty over your life. Though your circumstances may indeed be painful and difficult, they are not worthless. So muster the courage to say *yes* to your life, trusting that I am in control and I am with you in your struggles.

Come to Me with a courageous heart, hoping in Me, and I will bless you in many ways. Moreover, I will multiply your small act of bravery: *I will strengthen your heart.*

Be of good courage, and He shall
strengthen your heart, all you who hope
in the LORD. —Psalm 31:24 NKJV

"The cowardly, the unbelieving, the vile,
the murderers, the sexually immoral, those
who practice magic arts, the idolaters
and all liars—their place will be in the
fiery lake of burning sulfur. This is the
second death." —Revelation 21:8

See, the Sovereign LORD comes with power,
and his arm rules for him. See, his reward is
with him, and his recompense accompanies
him. He tends his flock like a shepherd: he
gathers the lambs in his arms and carries
them close to his heart; he gently leads
those that have young. —Isaiah 40:10–11

63

HOPE FOR WHAT YOU DO NOT SEE; eagerly wait for it with perseverance. Among the five senses, sight is often the one that people value the most. I created the world gloriously beautiful, and I want you to appreciate beauty when you see it. However, even more beneficial than sight is hope, which is itself a kind of vision. It enables you to see— through the eyes of your heart—things that are *not yet*. The most stunning example of this is the hope of heaven. Your ultimate destiny is to share in My Glory! This is My promise to you, secured through My finished work on the cross and My resurrection.

Practice hoping for things you do not see—both for this life and the next. Ask Me to guide you into hopes and dreams that are in line with My will. Train the eyes of your heart to "see" these blessings, while praying for My will to be done fully and only. Discipline yourself to *wait eagerly*—with your focus on Me and the longed-for outcome. Remain hopeful and expectant as you *wait with perseverance.*

*If we hope for what we do not
see, we eagerly wait for it with
perseverance.* —Romans 8:25 NKJV

*"The glory which You gave Me I have
given them, that they may be one just
as We are one."* —John 17:22 NKJV

*Now faith is the assurance (the confirmation,
the title deed) of the things [we] hope for,
being the proof of things [we] do not see
and the conviction of their reality [faith
perceiving as real fact what is not revealed
to the senses].* —Hebrews 11:1 AMP

64

DON'T BE AFRAID TO BE HAPPY. Because you are Mine, you can expect to experience some happiness—even in this broken world. Yet anxiety sometimes intrudes upon your carefree moments. You start wondering if there are things you should be doing or plans you should be making. Your underlying feeling is that it isn't safe to let down your guard and simply be happy in the moment. How wrong this is, My child!

I have called you to *cease striving*—let go, relax—*and know that I am God*. You may think that you need to have all your ducks in a row before you can relax and enjoy My Presence. But consider the overall context of this command: *though the earth give way and the mountains fall into the heart of the sea*. The psalmist who penned these words was describing a terrifying catastrophe. So you don't need to wait till you've solved all the problems in your life; this very moment is the right time to enjoy Me. Come boldly into My Presence, saying, "Jesus, I choose to enjoy You—here and now."

*Happy are the people whose God is
the L*ORD*! —Psalm 144:15* NKJV

*Cease striving and know that I am God; I
will be exalted among the nations, I will be
exalted in the earth. —Psalm 46:10* NASB

*God is our refuge and strength, an ever-
present help in trouble. Therefore we will
not fear, though the earth give way and the
mountains fall into the heart of the sea, though
its waters roar and foam and the mountains
quake with their surging. —Psalm 46:1–3*

65

YOU ARE *BEING RENEWED DAY BY DAY*. So do not be weighed down by yesterday's failures and disappointments. Begin this day anew, seeking to please Me and walk in My ways—focusing on today! As you do, I am able to transform you little by little. This is a lifelong process—a journey fraught with problems and pain. It is also a journey full of Joy and Peace because I am with you each step of the way.

Notice that you are *being* renewed. This is not something you can do by your effort and willpower alone. My Spirit is in charge of your renewal, and He is alive within you—directing your growth in grace. Do not be discouraged when you encounter problems and pain along your way. These are vital parts of the renewal process. Muster the courage to thank Me when you are going through painful experiences. Find hope through trusting that I continually *hold you by your right hand*—and I am preparing you for Glory!

We do not lose heart. Though our outer self is wasting away, our inner self is being renewed day by day. —2 Corinthians 4:16 ESV

You, however, are controlled not by the sinful nature but by the Spirit, if the Spirit of God lives in you. And if anyone does not have the Spirit of Christ, he does not belong to Christ. —Romans 8:9

Yet I am always with you; you hold me by my right hand. You guide me with your counsel, and afterward you will take me into glory. —Psalm 73:23–24

151

66

THERE IS AN OPEN ROAD AHEAD OF YOU—all the way
to heaven. I am your traveling Companion, and I know
every twist and turn of your path. You see problems and
limitations impeding your progress no matter which
direction you look. But your vision is ever so limited. All
I ask of you is to take the next small step—refusing to
give up, refusing to stop trusting Me.

Your life is truly a faith-walk, and I am absolutely
faithful! Though your understanding will fail you, I never
will. The challenge before you is to stop focusing on your
problems and limitations—and to believe that the way
ahead really is an *open* road, in spite of how it looks.

I am the Way to the Father in heaven. Remember how
much I had to suffer in order to open up *the path of Life*
for you. No one else will ever have to endure what I went
through. When you are struggling, simply take the next
step and thank Me for clearing the way before you—all
the way to heaven.

No temptation has seized you except what is common to man. And God is faithful; he will not let you be tempted beyond what you can bear. But when you are tempted, he will also provide a way out so that you can stand up under it. —1 Corinthians 10:13

We walk by faith, not by sight.
—2 Corinthians 5:7 NKJV

Jesus said to [Thomas], "I am the way, the truth, and the life. No one comes to the Father except through Me." —John 14:6 NKJV

You have made known to me the path of life; you will fill me with joy in your presence, with eternal pleasures at your right hand. —Psalm 16:11

It is impossible for that man to despair who remembers that his Helper is omnipotent.

JEREMY TAYLOR

O Sovereign
Lord! You made
the heavens and
earth by your
strong hand and
powerful arm.
Nothing is too
hard for you!

Jeremiah 32:17 nlt

67

YOU CAN FIND JOY IN THE MIDST OF BROKENNESS. One of the hardest times to be joyful is when you're dealing with multiple problems—seeking solutions but finding none—and then several new difficulties beset you. If you focus too much on finding solutions, you will sink under the weight of your problems. So it's vital to remember that I am present with you in adversity. I am at work in your situation, and My matchless wisdom enables Me to bring good out of evil—ultimately outsmarting evil with good!

The way to find Joy in adversity is to encounter *Me*. You can pray, "Jesus, help me find You in the midst of this mess!" As you unplug your emotions from all the problems and plug them into My Presence, good things start to happen. Your dark mood grows steadily lighter and brighter. Also, as you *remain in Me*—plugged in to My Presence—I enable you to see things from My perspective. You can be joyful in the midst of brokenness by staying connected to Me.

*My brethren, count it all joy when you fall into
various trials, knowing that the testing of your
faith produces patience.* —James 1:2–3 NKJV

*Oh, the depth of the riches of the
wisdom and knowledge of God! How
unsearchable his judgments, and his
paths beyond tracing out!* —Romans 11:33

*"Remain in me, and I will remain in you.
No branch can bear fruit by itself; it must
remain in the vine. Neither can you bear
fruit unless you remain in me."* —John 15:4

68

SEEKING TO PLEASE ME IS A JOYOUS WAY TO LIVE. Of course, *without faith it is impossible to please Me.* You must really *believe that I exist and that I reward those who earnestly seek Me.*

Living to please Me is a wise investment—not only for rewards in heaven but also for daily pleasure on earth. I am meant to be the Center of your existence, the Sun around which you orbit. When you live this way—enjoying Me, serving Me, desiring to please Me—you stay in your proper orbit. When you live in a self-centered way, you go off course.

The challenge is to keep Me central in what you do, say, and think. This battle begins in your mind, so work on *taking captive every thought to make it obedient to Me.* Study My Word to find out what pleases Me, and remember how wonderfully well I love you. Awareness of My amazing Love will help you stay in orbit around the Son—enjoying the radiant pleasures of My Presence.

And without faith it is impossible to please God, because anyone who comes to him must believe that he exists and that he rewards those who earnestly seek him. —Hebrews 11:6

We demolish arguments and every pretension that sets itself up against the knowledge of God, and we take captive every thought to make it obedient to Christ. —2 Corinthians 10:5

We . . . do not cease to pray for you, and ask . . . that you may walk worthy of the Lord, fully pleasing Him, being fruitful in every good work and increasing in the knowledge of God. —Colossians 1:9–10 NKJV

69

I MYSELF GO BEFORE YOU AND WILL BE WITH YOU. So do not be afraid; do not be discouraged. I, your loving Savior, am also infinite God! I am omnipresent: present everywhere at once. This makes it possible for Me to go ahead of you—opening up the way—without ever leaving your side.

The promise of My Presence is for all time. No matter where you go or what circumstances you encounter, I *will* be with you. This is the basis of your courage and confidence. Though fear and discouragement may sometimes slink into your heart, this is not their rightful home. Your heart is *My* dwelling place, and those hurtful emotions are not from Me. In fact, My *perfect Love casts out fear.* So check your heart from time to time, to see if fear and discouragement are loitering there. If you discover those unwelcome intruders, ask the Holy Spirit to function as a bouncer and boot them out! Then, encourage yourself with My promise to *go before you and be with you*—and let My perfect Love renew your hope.

The Lord himself goes before you and will be with you; he will never leave you nor forsake you. Do not be afraid; do not be discouraged. —Deuteronomy 31:8

I pray that out of his glorious riches he may strengthen you with power through his Spirit in your inner being, so that Christ may dwell in your hearts through faith. —Ephesians 3:16–17

There is no fear in love; but perfect love casts out fear, because fear involves punishment, and the one who fears is not perfected in love. —1 John 4:18 NASB

70

PRAISE WILL GET YOU VICTORIOUSLY through this day. When you worship Me, you connect with Me in a powerful way that transcends time and circumstances. I live in your praises, and *you live and move and have your being in Me.* Praising Me draws you into the depths of My Presence, where you can glimpse My Power and Glory.

Depression, fear, and self-pity vanish when you engage in heartfelt worship. The evil one and his demonic followers flee from these glorious strains. So it is wise to praise Me. However, the most important reason for worship is that I am *worthy to receive honor and glory and praise*! The Bible is full of commands to give Me praise.

No matter how dark and difficult your day may seem, the Light of My Presence will shine through the darkness as you worship Me. This glorifies Me and enables you to live above your circumstances—victoriously!

*Thou art holy, O thou that inhabitest
the praises of Israel.* —Psalm 22:3 KJV

*In Him we live and move and have our being,
as also some of your own poets have said, "For
we are also His offspring."* —Acts 17:28 NKJV

*Then I looked and heard the voice of
many angels, numbering thousands upon
thousands, and ten thousand times ten
thousand. They encircled the throne and
the living creatures and the elders. In a
loud voice they sang: "Worthy is the Lamb,
who was slain, to receive power and wealth
and wisdom and strength and honor and
glory and praise!"* —Revelation 5:11–12

71

GIVE YOUR ENTIRE ATTENTION to what I am doing right now, and don't get worked up about what may or may not happen tomorrow. This sounds so simple, but it goes against the grain of human nature—against the strong desire to feel in control. Mankind longs to be able to forecast the future, and some people peddle their "expertise" in this area to make money. But the future belongs to Me, so you don't need to worry about it.

Trying not to think about something is usually ineffective and counterproductive. The effort to stop thinking about the matter keeps you chained to those thoughts. However, you can break free by focusing your attention on Me and on what I am doing in your life. I am your living Savior, and I am always doing *new things.*

What keeps most people chained to future-thoughts is their fear of what tomorrow may bring—wondering whether they will be able to cope with it. But remember this: *I will help you deal with whatever hard things come up—when the time comes!*

"Give your entire attention to what God is doing right now, and don't get worked up about what may or may not happen tomorrow. God will help you deal with whatever hard things come up when the time comes." —Matthew 6:34 MSG

"The Spirit of the LORD is upon Me, because He has anointed Me to preach the gospel to the poor; He has sent Me to heal the brokenhearted, to proclaim liberty to the captives and recovery of sight to the blind, to set at liberty those who are oppressed." —Luke 4:18 NKJV

See, the former things have taken place, and new things I declare; before they spring into being I announce them to you. —Isaiah 42:9

72

LEAN ON ME as you face the circumstances of this day. Whether or not they realize it, all people lean on—depend on—*something*: physical strength, intelligence, beauty, wealth, achievements, family, friends, and so on. All of these are gifts from Me, to be enjoyed gratefully. However, relying on any of these things is risky because every one of them can let you down.

When your circumstances are challenging and you are feeling weak, you tend to obsess about how you are going to make it through the day. This wastes a lot of time and energy; it also distracts you from Me. Whenever this happens, ask Me to open your eyes so you can find Me in the moment. "See" Me standing nearby, with My strong arm extended toward you—offering you My help. Don't try to pretend that you have it all together or that you're stronger than you really are. Instead, lean hard on Me, letting Me bear most of your weight and help you with your problems. Rejoice in Me—*your Strength*—and worship while leaning on Me.

A man of many companions may come to ruin, but there is a friend who sticks closer than a brother. —Proverbs 18:24

But I will sing of your strength, in the morning I will sing of your love; for you are my fortress, my refuge in times of trouble. O my Strength, I sing praise to you; you, O God, are my fortress, my loving God. —Psalm 59:16–17

By faith Jacob, when he was dying, blessed each of the sons of Joseph, and worshiped, leaning on the top of his staff. —Hebrews 11:21 NKJV

God's Word says there's
no hopeless situation,
illness, marriage. . . .
Our hope is the anchor
of our soul . . . the
confident hope of
Jesus Christ's return!

DONALD BAKER
AND EMERY NESTER

We're depending on
GOD; he's everything we
need. What's more, our
hearts brim with joy
since we've taken for
our own his holy name.
Love us, GOD, with all
you've got—that's what
we're depending on.

PSALM 33:20–22 MSG

73

I WATCH OVER ALL WHO LOVE ME. Let this promise of My watch-care comfort you—especially during difficult days. This promise is for *you* because you love Me. Of course, it is not a matter of earning My protection by loving Me. However, those who belong to Me—and are under My watchful care—are the ones who love Me. This is a response to what I have done: *You love Me because I first loved you.*

In times of extreme danger and destruction, even courageous adults sometimes cry out for their parents' help. This is an instinctive response, flowing out of childhood memories. When people are afraid, they long to feel protected by someone who is bigger and stronger. Be assured that I am always watching over you—*like a shepherd watching over his flock.* Sometimes you may *feel* alone and unprotected. The remedy is to trust that I am with you and to start communicating with Me—pouring out your heart. Expressing yourself freely to Me will help you become aware of My watchful, loving Presence.

*The L*ORD *watches over all who love him, but all the wicked he will destroy. —Psalm 145:20*

*We love Him because He first loved us.
—1 John 4:19* NKJV

*Hear the word of the L*ORD*, O nations; proclaim it in distant coastlands: "He who scattered Israel will gather them and will watch over his flock like a shepherd." —Jeremiah 31:10*

Trust in Him at all times, you people; pour out your heart before Him; God is a refuge for us. —Psalm 62:8 NKJV

74

I AM THE ONE WHO KEEPS YOU SAFE. You tend to rely heavily on your thinking and planning, as if that is where your security lies. When you start to feel anxious about something, your mind goes into overdrive—searching for solutions, searching for security. All the while I am with you, *holding you by your right hand.*

Beware of *trusting in yourself*—which is foolish. Instead, *walk in wisdom* and you will be *kept safe.* The essence of wisdom is to trust in Me more than in yourself or other people. I stand ready to *guide you with My counsel*, so bring all your concerns to Me. When you are feeling confused, it may be helpful to write out your prayers, asking Me to show you the way forward. Then wait in My Presence, giving Me time to guide your mind while you focus on Me and My Word. You can whisper, "Jesus," to help you stay focused. My Name—representing all that I AM—is *a strong tower*; those who *run to it are safe.*

Yet I am always with you; you hold me by my right hand. You guide me with your counsel, and afterward you will take me into glory. Whom have I in heaven but you? And earth has nothing I desire besides you. My flesh and my heart may fail, but God is the strength of my heart and my portion forever. —Psalm 73:23–26

He who trusts in himself is a fool, but he who walks in wisdom is kept safe. —Proverbs 28:26

The name of the Lord is a strong tower; the righteous run to it and are safe. —Proverbs 18:10 NKJV

75

MY STEADFAST LOVE NEVER CEASES, My Mercies never come to an end; they are new every morning. I know how desperately you want to believe this—and how much you are struggling to do so. Today, the only things that seem endless are your problems and your pain. But I am *here*—tenderly present—ready to help you get safely through this day. Believing this truth can make the difference between coping and giving up in despair.

Some days, when things are going reasonably well, it is easy to trust in My steadfast Love. But when new, unexpected problems strike, trusting Me takes much more effort. At such times it can help to remember that you receive new Mercies every morning. When you are getting dressed, recall that I have clothed you in *garments of salvation.* Because you wear My *robe of righteousness,* you are on your way to heaven! This is an incredible act of Mercy—snatching you from the jaws of hell and putting you on the path to Glory. Nothing you face today can compare with this mercy-gift of eternal Life!

The steadfast love of the LORD never ceases, his mercies never come to an end; they are new every morning; great is your faithfulness. —Lamentations 3:22–23 NRSV

I will greatly rejoice in the LORD, my soul shall be joyful in my God; for He has clothed me with the garments of salvation, He has covered me with the robe of righteousness, as a bridegroom decks himself with ornaments, and as a bride adorns herself with her jewels. —Isaiah 61:10 NKJV

"For God so loved the world, that he gave his only Son, that whoever believes in him should not perish but have eternal life." —John 3:16 ESV

76

WORRY IS LARGELY A MATTER of thinking about things at the wrong time. I have built into your brain the amazing capacity to observe your own thoughts. So it is possible to monitor your thoughts and make choices about them.

To avoid wasting mental and emotional energy, timing is very important. If you think about certain things at the wrong time—for example, when you're lying in bed—it's all too easy to start worrying about them. This is why it's so helpful to monitor your thinking. Instead of waiting until you're deep in worry, you can interrupt anxious thoughts and change the subject.

I want you to discipline your mind to minimize worry and maximize worship. This will require much ongoing effort, but you'll find that it's a path to freedom. When you realize you're thinking about something at the wrong time—a worrisome thought at a time when you can do nothing about it—take swift action. Tell yourself, "Not now!" and direct your mind elsewhere. The best direction for your thinking is toward Me. Draw near Me by expressing your trust in Me, your love for Me. This is worship.

*Then Jesus said to his disciples: "Therefore I
tell you, do not worry about your life, what
you will eat; or about your body, what you
will wear. Life is more than food, and the body
more than clothes. Consider the ravens: They
do not sow or reap, they have no storeroom
or barn; yet God feeds them. And how much
more valuable you are than birds! Who of you
by worrying can add a single hour to his life?
Since you cannot do this very little thing, why
do you worry about the rest?" —Luke 12:22–26*

*Worship Him who made heaven
and earth, the sea and springs of
water. —Revelation 14:7* NKJV

77

I WILL *FILL YOU WITH JOY AND PEACE* as you wait in My Presence. Spending time with Me demonstrates that you really do trust Me. People who trust mainly in themselves and their own abilities often crowd Me out of their lives. As you learn to trust Me more, you increasingly delight in time spent with Me. And the more you wait in My Presence, the deeper your faith grows—increasing your Joy and Peace.

Because you belong to Me, My Spirit lives in you. You may sometimes be unaware of His Presence, but He is always aware of you. Moreover, He is continually at work within you—*transforming you into My likeness with ever-increasing Glory.* You cooperate in this process by focusing on Me. As you become more and more like Me, hope grows within you. With the Spirit's help, this hope can well up inside you till it overflows—spilling out and splashing into the lives of other people!

*May the God of hope fill you with all joy
and peace as you trust in him, so that
you may overflow with hope by the power
of the Holy Spirit.* —Romans 15:13

*You will keep him in perfect peace,
whose mind is stayed on You, because
he trusts in You.* —Isaiah 26:3 NKJV

*You, however, are controlled not by the sinful
nature but by the Spirit, if the Spirit of God lives
in you. And if anyone does not have the Spirit of
Christ, he does not belong to Christ.* —Romans 8:9

*We, who with unveiled faces all reflect the Lord's
glory, are being transformed into his likeness
with ever-increasing glory, which comes from the
Lord, who is the Spirit.* —2 Corinthians 3:18

78

SING TO ME, *because I have dealt bountifully with you.*
When singing praises is the last thing you feel like doing,
it is probably just what you need. I have indeed been gracious in My dealings with you—whether or not it seems
that way. You have been on an uphill journey for a long
time, and you are growing weary. You yearn for some easy
days, for a path that is not so steep. But it is the strenuous
climbs that take you ever upward—closer and closer to
the summit.

The difficulty of your life circumstances is *not* a mistake! It's a matter of My Sovereign will and—to some
extent—your own goals. You desire to live close to Me
and to grow more fully into the one I created you to be.
Pursuing these goals has put you on an adventurous trail
where difficulties and dangers abound. Sometimes you
compare your journey with those of your friends who
seem to be on easier paths. But you cannot fully comprehend the problems they face. Nor do you know what the
future holds for them. Remember My response to Simon
Peter when he asked about My dealings with John: *"What
is that to you? You follow Me!"*

I will sing to the LORD, because He has dealt bountifully with me. —Psalm 13:6 NKJV

God is my strong fortress; and He sets the blameless in His way. He makes my feet like hinds' feet, and sets me on high places. —2 Samuel 22:33–34 NASB

Jesus said to [Peter], "If I want [John] to remain until I come, what is that to you? You follow Me!" —John 21:22 NASB

The word *hope* I
take for faith; and
indeed, hope is
nothing else but
the constancy
of faith.

JOHN CALVIN

*I have set the
Lord continually
before me; because
He is at my right
hand, I shall
not be moved.*

PSALM 16:8 AMP

79

REJOICE IN ME ALWAYS. *Let your gentleness be evident to all. I am near.* Rejoicing in Me can protect you from the temptation to complain. When your circumstances are stressful, it is easy for you to become irritable. But I want you to demonstrate gentleness—not irritability. This is possible to the extent that you find Joy in Me. Since I am *the same yesterday, today, and forever,* there is *always* much for you to rejoice about.

You can be joyful in the knowledge that *I am near.* When a man and a woman are deeply in love, they often bring out the best in each other. Just being near the beloved can soothe irritations and increase happiness. I am the Lover who is *always* nearby—unseen yet tenderly present. I can soothe your frustrations and fill you with Joy as you tune in to My loving Presence. One way to do this is to thank Me for My continual Presence and My constant Love. When circumstances are getting you down, turn your attention to Me and *consider the great Love* I have for you. Rejoice!

Rejoice in the Lord always. I will say it again: Rejoice! Let your gentleness be evident to all. The Lord is near. —Philippians 4:4–5

The fruit of the Spirit is love, joy, peace, patience, kindness, goodness, faithfulness, gentleness, self-control; against such things there is no law. —Galatians 5:22–23 ESV

Jesus Christ is the same yesterday, today, and forever. —Hebrews 13:8 NKJV

Whoever is wise, let him heed these things and consider the great love of the LORD. —Psalm 107:43

80

YOU ARE BEING TRANSFORMED into *My image from Glory to Glory.* Trust My Spirit to do this massive work in you. Yield to My ways, wisdom, and will. When life gets tough, don't waste those hard circumstances. Instead, ask Me to use them to transform you more and more into My likeness—helping you become your true self. You must be willing to *share in My sufferings so that you may also share in My Glory.*

Though your troubles may seem heavy and endless, they are actually *light and momentary*—compared to the *eternal Glory* they are achieving for you. This is why it is reasonable and right to thank Me for hard times, to praise Me for ongoing troubles. This serves a dual purpose: When you give thanks in the midst of adversity—because of who I am and what I have done for you—I am glorified. And your thankfulness helps you make progress in your transformation *from Glory to Glory.*

We all, with unveiled face, beholding as in a mirror the glory of the Lord, are being transformed into the same image from glory to glory, just as by the Spirit of the Lord. —2 Corinthians 3:18 NKJV

Now if we are children, then we are heirs— heirs of God and co-heirs with Christ, if indeed we share in his sufferings in order that we may also share in his glory. —Romans 8:17

Our light and momentary troubles are achieving for us an eternal glory that far outweighs them all. —2 Corinthians 4:17

Speak to one another with psalms, hymns and spiritual songs. Sing and make music in your heart to the Lord, always giving thanks to God the Father for everything, in the name of our Lord Jesus Christ. —Ephesians 5:19–20

81

REMEMBER ME ON YOUR BED; *think of Me through the watches of the night.* When you are wakeful during the night, thoughts can fly at you from all directions. Unless you take charge of them, you are likely to become anxious. Your best strategy is to think about *Me* during your night watches. Start communicating with Me about whatever is on your mind. *Cast all your anxiety on Me because I care for you.* I am taking care of you! This makes it possible for you to relax and *rejoice in the shadow of My wings.*

When you remember Me during the night, think about who I really am. Ponder My perfections: My Love, Joy, and Peace. Rejoice in My majesty, wisdom, grace, and mercy. Find comfort in My names: Shepherd, Savior, Immanuel, Prince of Peace. Be awed by My Power and Glory, for I am King of kings and Lord of lords. Thus you worship Me and enjoy My Presence. These thoughts of Me will clear your mind—helping you see things from My perspective—and refresh your entire being.

On my bed I remember you; I think of you through the watches of the night. —Psalm 63:6

Cast all your anxiety on [God] because he cares for you. —1 Peter 5:7

Because You have been my help, therefore in the shadow of Your wings I will rejoice. —Psalm 63:7 NKJV

Fight the good fight of the faith. Take hold of the eternal life to which you were called. . . . I charge you to keep this command without spot or blame until the appearing of our Lord Jesus Christ, which God will bring about in his own time—God, the blessed and only Ruler, the King of kings and Lord of lords, who alone is immortal and who lives in unapproachable light, whom no one has seen or can see. To him be honor and might forever. —1 Timothy 6:12, 14–16

82

TRUST ME IN TIMES OF CONFUSION—when things don't make sense and nothing you do seems to help. This type of trust delights Me because I know it is real. Invite Me to enter into your struggles—to be ever so close to you. Though other people may not really understand what you're going through, I understand perfectly. Find comfort in knowing you're not alone in your struggles. *I am with you, watching over you* continually.

Long-term trials can drain you of energy and hope, making it hard for you to keep trusting Me. But I have given you a wonderful *Helper*, the Holy Spirit, who never runs out of strength. You can ask for His help, praying: "I trust You, Jesus; help me, Holy Spirit." Instead of trying to resolve all your problems, simply rest in My Presence. Trust that there is a way forward, even though you can't yet see it. I am providing a good way for you, though it is bumpy at times. When the road is rough, cling all the more tightly to Me. As *your soul clings to Me, My right hand upholds you.*

I am with you and will watch over you
wherever you go, and I will bring you back to
this land. I will not leave you until I have done
what I have promised you. —Genesis 28:15

"When the Helper comes, whom I shall
send to you from the Father, the Spirit of
truth who proceeds from the Father, He
will testify of Me." —John 15:26 NKJV

My soul clings to you; your right
hand upholds me. —Psalm 63:8

83

I EMPOWER YOU—*infusing inner strength into you* so that you are *ready for anything and equal to anything.* It's essential to remember that this inner strength comes *through Me*, through your connection with Me. It comes to you as you need it—as you take trusting steps of dependence, moving forward with your eyes on Me. This promise is a powerful antidote to fear—especially your fear of being overwhelmed by circumstances you see looming ahead. They may look daunting, but in Me you are indeed *ready for anything and equal to anything.*

Of course, you're not *currently* ready for every imaginable situation. I carefully control what happens in your life. I am constantly protecting you from both known and unknown dangers. And I provide strength, just when you need it, for everything I allow to touch your life. Many of the future things you anxiously anticipate will not actually reach you. My promise is for things you face in the present, and it is sufficient. So when you are feeling the strain of an uphill journey, tell yourself the truth: *"I have strength for all things through Christ who empowers me!"*

I have strength for all things in Christ Who empowers me [I am ready for anything and equal to anything through Him Who infuses inner strength into me; I am self-sufficient in Christ's sufficiency]. —Philippians 4:13 AMP

"Abide in Me, and I in you. As the branch cannot bear fruit of itself, unless it abides in the vine, neither can you, unless you abide in Me." —John 15:4 NKJV

The LORD is my strength and my shield; my heart trusts in him, and I am helped. My heart leaps for joy and I will give thanks to him in song. —Psalm 28:7

84

WAIT IN HOPE FOR ME; I am your Help and your Shield. Waiting in itself is not a virtue. The important thing is *how* you wait: in a resigned, impatient way or *in hope*—keeping your focus on Me. One aspect of hope is confident expectation. When your overarching hope is *for Me*, you have every reason to be confident. I have promised to be *with you always, even to the end of the age.* Moreover, at the end of time, I am coming back in glorious Power to judge the world and establish My kingdom.

While you are waiting, remember that *I am your Help and your Shield.* My unfailing Love guarantees that I am always available to help you. You access this loving help through your trust in Me. No matter what is happening or how bad you feel, voice your trust in Me! I have shielded you from many hardships, and I will continue to protect you. So put your hope fully in Me, and the Light of My Presence will shine into your waiting times.

We wait in hope for the LORD; he is our help and our shield. —Psalm 33:20

And Jesus came and spoke to them, saying, "All authority has been given to Me in heaven and on earth. Go therefore and make disciples of all the nations, baptizing them in the name of the Father and of the Son and of the Holy Spirit, teaching them to observe all things that I have commanded you; and lo, I am with you always, even to the end of the age." —Matthew 28:18–20 NKJV

But I am like an olive tree flourishing in the house of God; I trust in God's unfailing love for ever and ever. —Psalm 52:8

I am your risen, living Savior! Through My resurrection you have been born again to an ever-living hope. It is vital for you to remain hopeful, no matter what is going on in your life. . . . When storms break upon your life, you can find only one adequate source of help—Me!

Jesus Lives

*"The L*ORD* is my portion," says my soul, "therefore I have hope in Him."*

LAMENTATIONS 3:24 NASB

85

BLESSED ARE THE POOR IN SPIRIT, for theirs is the king-dom of heaven. So when you're acutely aware of your insufficiency—rejoice! This is what being *poor in spirit* is all about. The world applauds self-sufficiency, and book-stores abound with volumes designed to help you reach this goal. However, this is not the way of My kingdom. I want My children to recognize and rejoice in their utter dependence on Me.

You have been saved by grace, through faith. Both grace and faith are gifts! Your part is to be receptive and responsive to these glorious gifts. The best response is gratitude—a heart overflowing with thankfulness for all I have done. You are exceedingly blessed because the kingdom of heaven is yours. When the strain of living in this fallen world is getting you down, resist the tempta-tion to feel sorry for yourself. Instead, say to yourself, "I am blessed and thankful—and on my way *to Glory*!"

"Blessed are the poor in spirit, for theirs is the kingdom of heaven." —Matthew 5:3 NKJV

For it is by grace you have been saved, through faith—and this not from yourselves, it is the gift of God. —Ephesians 2:8

Thanks be to God for his indescribable gift! —2 Corinthians 9:15

You will guide me with Your counsel, and afterward receive me to glory. —Psalm 73:24 NKJV

86

I AM THE LIGHT OF THE WORLD. My followers *will not walk in darkness, but will have the Light of Life.* Even though there is much darkness in this world, you always have access to Me. So you are never in total darkness. The trail before you may look obscure, especially as it disappears into the future. You would like it to be floodlit so you could anticipate what's up ahead. But I tell you: I am enough! I am with you, and I also go before you— illuminating the way. Your assignment is to trust Me and follow the Light I provide. No matter how dim it may seem, it is sufficient for your journey through today.

Someday you will be with Me in heaven, and there you will see My Light in all its Glory. Darkness will be a thing of the past, and you will see everything clearly. *There will be no more night. You will not need the light of a lamp or of the sun, for I will give you Light*—beyond anything you can imagine! Live close to Me, and you *will have the Light of Life.*

Then Jesus spoke to them again, saying, "I am the light of the world. He who follows Me shall not walk in darkness, but have the light of life." —John 8:12 NKJV

The path of the righteous is like the first gleam of dawn, shining ever brighter till the full light of day. —Proverbs 4:18

There will be no more night. [People in heaven] will not need the light of a lamp or the light of the sun, for the Lord God will give them light. And they will reign for ever and ever. —Revelation 22:5

87

I AM *A VERY PRESENT AND WELL-PROVED HELP in trouble.*
My Presence is always with you, but I am *very* present in
times of distress. Because you are a member of My royal
family—a citizen of My heavenly kingdom—I am committed to caring for you. During stressful times, your
heart may race and your adrenaline level may soar. These
physiological changes can block your awareness of My
Presence. So it's vital at such times to remind yourself:
"Jesus is here with me; in fact, He is *very present* with
me in this hard situation." Then, take some slow, deep
breaths so you can relax enough to connect with Me and
draw strength from Me.

Biblical history has many examples of My faithfulness
during times of trouble. World history—including current
events—also contains proof of My powerful Presence. You
won't hear of this in secular news reports, but I continue to
do miracles in your world. Moreover, as you look back over
the years of your own life, you will see many instances of
My meeting *your* needs in hard times. Since I am such a
well-proved Help, you can trust Me to help you now!

*God is our Refuge and Strength [mighty
and impenetrable to temptation], a
very present and well-proved help
in trouble.* —Psalm 46:1 AMP

*The LORD your God dried up the Jordan before
you until you had crossed over. The LORD
your God did to the Jordan just what he had
done to the Red Sea when he dried it up before
us until we had crossed over.* —Joshua 4:23

*To him who is able to keep you from falling
and to present you before his glorious
presence without fault and with great
joy—to the only God our Savior be glory,
majesty, power and authority, through
Jesus Christ our Lord, before all ages,
now and forevermore!* —Jude 24–25

88

WORSHIP ME IN THE BEAUTY OF HOLINESS. There is a great deal of beauty in your world, but none of it is perfectly holy. So *the beauty of holiness* is something you know only in part—for now. Someday *you will know fully, even as you are fully known.* Even now, though, awareness of My holiness stimulates worship. Pondering My perfection—untainted by even a speck of sin—delights you and fills you with awe. I invite you to join with the angels in proclaiming: *"Holy, holy, holy is the Lord of hosts; the whole earth is full of His Glory!"*

Worshiping Me well transforms you—changing you more and more into the one I designed you to be. Genuine worship requires that you know Me as I truly am. You cannot comprehend Me perfectly or completely, but you *can* strive to know Me accurately, as I am revealed in the Bible. By deepening your understanding of Me, you are transformed and I am glorified—in beautiful worship.

Give unto the LORD the glory due to His name; worship the LORD in the beauty of holiness. —Psalm 29:2 NKJV

Now we see but a poor reflection as in a mirror; then we shall see face to face. Now I know in part; then I shall know fully, even as I am fully known. —1 Corinthians 13:12

One [seraphim] cried to another and said: "Holy, holy, holy is the LORD of hosts; the whole earth is full of His glory!" —Isaiah 6:3 NKJV

89

I HAVE CALLED YOU BY NAME; you are Mine. No matter how isolated you may sometimes feel, you belong to Me! I have redeemed you by paying the full penalty for your sins. *Nothing can separate you from My loving Presence.* I called you to Myself in the most personal way: reaching down into the circumstances of your life, speaking into the intricacies of your heart and mind. Although I have vast numbers of followers, you are not a number to Me. I always speak to you *by name.* In fact, you are so precious to Me that *I have inscribed you on the palms of My hands.*

When world events are swirling around you and your personal world feels unsteady, don't let your mind linger on those stressors. Tell yourself the truth: "Yes, this world is full of trouble, but Jesus is with me and He is in control." It is this *but Jesus* factor that makes all the difference in your life. Change the subject from problems to My Presence many times daily by whispering, "But Jesus . . ." and looking to Me.

The Lord who created you, O Israel, says:
Don't be afraid, for I have ransomed
you; I have called you by name; you
are mine. —Isaiah 43:1 TLB

I am convinced that neither death nor life,
neither angels nor demons, neither the
present nor the future, nor any powers,
neither height nor depth, nor anything
else in all creation, will be able to separate
us from the love of God that is in Christ
Jesus our Lord. —Romans 8:38–39

See, I have inscribed you on the palms
of My hands; your walls are continually
before Me. —Isaiah 49:16 NKJV

90

I—THE SOVEREIGN LORD—AM YOUR STRENGTH. You are keenly aware of your weakness. You know that your strength is insufficient to handle the many challenges you face. Though this feels uncomfortable, it is actually a very blessed place to be. Awareness of your neediness can help you keep turning to Me, letting Me *supply all your need according to My riches in Glory.*

When your energy is running low, connect with Me—*your Strength.* Sometimes I pour abundant energy into you as you spend time in My Presence. At other times I energize you only bit by bit, giving you just enough strength to keep moving slowly forward. Although the abundant provision is more dramatic and satisfying, do not be discouraged when I choose to give you strength sufficient only for the moment. This may be My way of keeping you ever so close to Me on your life-path, leaning on Me. This closeness helps you hear My whispers—telling you of My delight in you. To hear these whispers clearly, you must trust that I, *the Sovereign Lord,* am in charge of your life and that your journey—though difficult—is full of blessing.

The Sovereign LORD is my strength; he makes my feet like the feet of a deer, he enables me to go on the heights. —Habakkuk 3:19

My God shall supply all your need according to His riches in glory by Christ Jesus. —Philippians 4:19 NKJV

Splendor and majesty are before him; strength and glory are in his sanctuary. Ascribe to the LORD, O families of nations, ascribe to the LORD glory and strength. —Psalm 96:6–7

Hope is one
of the principal
springs that keep
mankind in motion.

Thomas Fuller

Though you have
made me see
troubles, many
and bitter, you
will restore my
life again. . . . You
will increase my
honor and comfort
me once again.

Psalm 71:20–21

91

I AM CALLING YOU to live in joyful dependence on Me. Many people view dependence as a despicable condition, so they strive to be as self-sufficient as possible. This is not My way for you! I designed you to need Me continually—and to delight in that neediness. When you live in harmony with your Creator's intentions for you, you can maximize your potential and enjoy your life more.

The apostle Paul exhorted Christians to *be joyful always* and to *pray continually*. There is always Joy to be found in My Presence, and I have promised I will *not leave you or forsake you*. So you can speak to Me at all times, knowing that I hear and I care. Praying continually is a way of demonstrating your deliberate dependence on Me—the One to whom you pray. Another powerful way of relying on Me is studying My Word, asking Me to use it to transform you through and through. These delightful disciplines help you live in joyful dependence on Me. *Delight yourself in Me* more and more; this increases your Joy and glorifies Me.

Be joyful always; pray continually.
—1 Thessalonians 5:16–17

The LORD, He is the One who goes before
you. He will be with you, He will not leave
you nor forsake you; do not fear nor be
dismayed. —Deuteronomy 31:8 NKJV

With my whole heart I have sought You; oh, let
me not wander from Your commandments! Your
word I have hidden in my heart, that I might not
sin against You. Blessed are You, O LORD! Teach
me Your statutes. —Psalm 119:10–12 NKJV

Delight yourself in the LORD and he will give
you the desires of your heart. —Psalm 37:4

92

WALK IN THE LIGHT OF MY PRESENCE—rejoicing in My Name all day long, exulting in My righteousness. This world is increasingly dark, but the Light of My Presence is as bright as ever. In fact, My Glory shines more vividly against the dark backdrop of evil. When Christlike goodness collides with worldly vileness, be on the lookout for miracles! This collision of spiritual opposites creates atmospheric conditions that are conducive to My powerful interventions.

No matter how difficult your circumstances may be, you can still *rejoice in My Name.* The essence of all that I am is distilled into this one word: *Jesus.* You can use My Name as a whispered prayer, as a praise, as a protection—and it never loses its potency. Even in the darkest situations, you can *exult*—rejoice jubilantly—*in My righteousness!* Nothing can tarnish this righteousness, which I have woven into shining *garments of salvation* for you to wear forever. This is how you walk in My Light: by making full use of My holy Name and by wearing *the robe of righteousness* joyfully.

Blessed are those who have learned to acclaim you, who walk in the light of your presence, O LORD. They rejoice in your name all day long; they exult in your righteousness. —Psalm 89:15–16

Therefore God exalted him to the highest place and gave him the name that is above every name, that at the name of Jesus every knee should bow, in heaven and on earth and under the earth, and every tongue confess that Jesus Christ is Lord, to the glory of God the Father. —Philippians 2:9–11

I will greatly rejoice in the LORD, my soul shall be joyful in my God; for He has clothed me with the garments of salvation, He has covered me with the robe of righteousness, as a bridegroom decks himself with ornaments, and as a bride adorns herself with her jewels. —Isaiah 61:10 NKJV

215

93

I AM A SHIELD FOR ALL WHO TAKE REFUGE IN ME. So come close to Me and hover under the umbrella of My shielding Presence.

You sometimes feel unprotected and exposed to dangers. This happens when you crawl out from under My protective Presence and try to face the world on your own. You do this unconsciously, whenever you forget the essential truth that I am with you. The fear you feel at such times can alert you to what has happened, and the remedy is simple: *Take refuge in Me.*

Shielding you from dangers is part of My job description because *I am your Shepherd.* I am vigilant, and I know exactly what is on the path ahead of you. I anticipate perilous situations and prepare you for them. A masterful shepherd can often take care of trouble so skillfully that his sheep remain blissfully unaware of it. So it is wise to choose carefully the one whom you will follow—your "shepherd." I am the only absolutely *Good Shepherd.* Follow Me and My ways; let Me protect you from danger *and* from fear.

As for God, his way is perfect; the word of the Lord is flawless. He is a shield for all who take refuge in him. —2 Samuel 22:31

The Lord is my shepherd, I shall not be in want. He makes me lie down in green pastures, he leads me beside quiet waters, he restores my soul. He guides me in paths of righteousness for his name's sake. Even though I walk through the valley of the shadow of death, I will fear no evil, for you are with me; your rod and your staff, they comfort me. —Psalm 23:1–4

"I am the good shepherd. The good shepherd gives His life for the sheep. . . . I am the good shepherd; and I know My sheep, and am known by My own. As the Father knows Me, even so I know the Father; and I lay down My life for the sheep." —John 10:11, 14–15 NKJV

94

I CALL YOU TO *LEAD THE LIFE* that I have assigned to you, and to be content. Beware of comparing your situation with that of someone else—and feeling dissatisfied because of the comparison. It is also harmful to compare your circumstances with what they used to be or with fantasies that bear little resemblance to reality. Instead, make every effort to accept as your *calling* the life I have assigned to you. This perspective helps take the sting out of even the harshest circumstances. If I have called you to a situation, I will give you everything you need to endure it—and even to find Joy in the midst of it.

Learning to be content is both a discipline and an art: You train your mind to trust My sovereign ways with you—bowing before My mysterious, infinite intelligence. You search for Me in the details of your day, all the while looking for good to emerge from trouble and confusion. You accept the way things are without losing hope for a better future. And you rejoice in the hope of heaven, knowing that indescribably joyful Life is your *ultimate* calling!

*Let each person lead the life that the Lord
has assigned to him, and to which God
has called him. This is my rule in all the
churches. —1 Corinthians 7:17 ESV*

*I know what it is to be in need, and I know what
it is to have plenty. I have learned the secret
of being content in any and every situation,
whether well fed or hungry, whether living
in plenty or in want. —Philippians 4:12*

*Oh, the depth of the riches of the wisdom and
knowledge of God! How unsearchable his
judgments, and his paths beyond tracing out!
"Who has known the mind of the Lord? Or who
has been his counselor?" "Who has ever given to
God, that God should repay him?" For from him
and through him and to him are all things. To
him be the glory forever! —Romans 11:33–36*

95

I GIVE STRENGTH TO MY PEOPLE; I bless My people with Peace. "My people" are all those who trust Me as their Savior-God. My death on the cross for your sins was sufficient to provide *everlasting Life* because I am truly God. So rest assured that the One who provides eternal Life will also give you strength.

When you are feeling weak, don't waste energy worrying about whether you can cope with the challenges you face. I know better than you what is on the path before you, and I stand ready to help—every step of the way. Having bought you with My own blood, I have a huge vested interest in you.

Because you are Mine, I want to bless you with My Peace. The Peace I give you is *not as the world gives*; it can coexist with the most difficult situations because it is transcendent. It rises above both your circumstances and your understanding—and it can lift *you* up too!

The Lord gives strength to his people; the Lord blesses his people with peace. —Psalm 29:11

"For God so loved the world that He gave His only begotten Son, that whoever believes in Him should not perish but have everlasting life." —John 3:16 NKJV

"Peace I leave with you, My peace I give to you; not as the world gives do I give to you. Let not your heart be troubled, neither let it be afraid." —John 14:27 NKJV

The peace of God, which transcends all understanding, will guard your hearts and your minds in Christ Jesus. —Philippians 4:7

221

96

YOU ARE ON AN ADVENTUROUS TRAIL WITH Me. This is not an easy time, but it is nonetheless good—full of blessings as well as struggles. Be open to learning all that I want to teach you as you journey through challenging terrain. And be willing to let go of familiar comforts so you can say a wholehearted "Yes!" to this adventure.

I will give you everything you need to cope with the challenges you face. Don't waste energy projecting yourself into the future—trying to walk through those "not yet" times in your mind. This is a form of unbelief. I have unlimited resources to provide what you need, including a vast army of angels at My beck and call.

Pray continually as you make decisions about this journey. I can help you make wise choices because I know everything—including what lies ahead on your path. Your mind makes various plans about your way, but I am the One who *directs your steps and makes them sure.*

*The secret things belong to the Lord
our God, but those things which are
revealed belong to us and to our children
forever, that we may do all the words of
this law. —Deuteronomy 29:29 NKJV*

*For he will command his angels
concerning you to guard you in all your
ways; they will lift you up in their hands,
so that you will not strike your foot
against a stone. —Psalm 91:11–12*

Pray continually. —1 Thessalonians 5:17

*A man's mind plans his way, but
the Lord directs his steps and makes
them sure. —Proverbs 16:9 AMP*

Our hope is not
hung upon such an
untwisted thread as,
"I imagine so," or
"It is likely." . . . Our
salvation is fastened
with God's own hand,
and with Christ's
own strength, to the
strong stake of God's
unchangeable nature.

SAMUEL RUTHERFORD

*"I am the LORD, and
I do not change."*

MALACHI 3:6 NLT

97

KEEP RETURNING YOUR FOCUS TO ME! *I am always thinking about you and watching everything that concerns you.* You, however, are only human, and you will lose sight of Me at times. I know how hard it is for you to stay focused on Me, especially when you are feeling weak or weary. So give yourself grace whenever you realize your mind and heart have wandered from Me. And waste no time in returning to Me by praising Me in thought, word, or song. Even whispering My Name—reverently, lovingly—can be worship.

Let Me have all your worries and cares. This may sound easy, but it is not; you are accustomed to worry-thoughts roaming freely in your brain. So you must train yourself to bring all your cares into My Presence, trusting Me to help you. Remember that you are never alone in your struggles: I am *always* aware of you and your circumstances. I can help you because *I have all authority in heaven and on earth.* As you come into My Presence, let go of your worries and cares—so you can cling to Me in childlike trust.

Let [God] have all your worries and cares, for he is always thinking about you and watching everything that concerns you. —1 Peter 5:7 TLB

Jesus came and spoke to [the disciples], saying, "All authority has been given to Me in heaven and on earth." —Matthew 28:18 NKJV

At that time the disciples came to Jesus and asked, "Who is the greatest in the kingdom of heaven?" He called a little child and had him stand among them. And he said: "I tell you the truth, unless you change and become like little children, you will never enter the kingdom of heaven. Therefore, whoever humbles himself like this child is the greatest in the kingdom of heaven." —Matthew 18:1–4

98

MY UNFAILING LOVE IS YOUR "FUEL"—the best source of
energy for you. This glorious source of strength is limitless, so it is always abundantly available. You tend to get
quite focused on your health and energy. There is a place
for such concerns, but they can occupy more and more of
your thoughts. When you are preoccupied with the condition of your body, I slip from the center of your mind
to the periphery. At such times, you are unable to receive
much help from Me. The remedy is to repent quickly—
turning away from obsessive thinking and turning
wholeheartedly toward Me.

The more you focus on Me, the more access you have
to My unfailing Love. This supernatural source of energy
flows through you freely as you look to Me in trust. Not
only does this increase your energy level; it also provides
a pathway for Me to love other people *through you*. So let
My limitless Love energize and empower you as you walk
along your life-path close to Me.

The LORD loves righteousness and justice; the earth is full of his unfailing love. —Psalm 33:5

Rejoice in the Lord always. Again I will say, rejoice! —Philippians 4:4 NKJV

To this end I labor, struggling with all his energy, which so powerfully works in me. —Colossians 1:29

Whoever confesses that Jesus is the Son of God, God abides in him, and he in God. And we have known and believed the love that God has for us. God is love, and he who abides in love abides in God, and God in him. —1 John 4:15–16 NKJV

99

I HAVE GOOD PLANS FOR YOU: I offer you *hope and a future*. Many people fear the future, but ultimately yours is glorious—beyond anything you can imagine! Knowing that you are on your way to heaven is immensely important for your well-being. This knowledge can help you every day, every moment of your life. Though your residence in paradise is in the future, heavenly Light transcends time and shines upon you even in the present.

Because I paid the penalty for your sins, I am your Hope—and I will never let you down. No matter what is happening in your life, it is still realistic to *hope in Me*. If you persist in trusting Me no matter what, *you will again praise Me for the help of My Presence.* Moreover, you can anticipate, via faith, the blessing that is ahead of you and start praising Me even in the dark. As you keep looking to Me in hope, My heavenly Light shines more brightly in your heart. This is *the Light of the knowledge of My Glory*!

*"For I know the plans I have for you,"
declares the LORD, "plans to prosper you
and not to harm you, plans to give you
hope and a future."* —Jeremiah 29:11

*Why are you in despair, O my soul? And why
have you become disturbed within me? Hope
in God, for I shall again praise Him for the
help of His presence.* —Psalm 42:5 NASB

*It is the God who commanded light to
shine out of darkness, who has shone in
our hearts to give the light of the knowledge
of the glory of God in the face of Jesus
Christ.* —2 Corinthians 4:6 NKJV

100

THE WORLD ABOUNDS with negative things to think about. Sometimes problems—yours or others'—seem to shout for your attention. They can occupy more and more of your thinking, causing you to *become weary and discouraged in your soul.* But remember: You can *choose* the subject of your thoughts. Cry out to Me and I will help you. Turn toward Me, letting My Light shine upon you.

Do not be defeated by wrong choices you have made in the past. And don't let past decisions define who you are in the present. Each moment provides a fresh opportunity to draw near Me and enjoy My Presence. One way to do this is to pray, "Jesus, I choose to seek *You* in the midst of my problems." Refuse to get discouraged, even if you have to say this hundreds of times daily. *In this world you will have trouble. But take heart! I have overcome the world.* You can find Peace in Me.

Consider Him who endured such hostility from sinners against Himself, lest you become weary and discouraged in your souls. —Hebrews 12:3 NKJV

This poor man cried out, and the LORD heard him, and saved him out of all his troubles. The angel of the LORD encamps all around those who fear Him, and delivers them. —Psalm 34:6–7 NKJV

"I have told you these things, so that in me you may have peace. In this world you will have trouble. But take heart! I have overcome the world." —John 16:33

101

TAKE TIME TO *MEDITATE ON MY UNFAILING LOVE. For I am your God forever and ever; I will be your Guide even to the end.* Ask the Holy Spirit to help you meditate on My loving Presence—to bring your mind back to Me whenever it wanders. Encourage yourself with the words of the patriarch Jacob: *"Surely the Lord is in this place."* Rejoice that I am your God forevermore—today, tomorrow, and throughout all eternity.

I am also your Guide. It is easy to be spooked by the future when you forget that I am leading you each step along your life-path. Ever since you trusted Me as Savior, My guiding Presence has been available to you. I am training you to be increasingly aware of Me as you go about your daily activities. You can draw near Me at any time simply by whispering My Name. Later, when you have more time, bring Me *your prayer and supplication with thanksgiving.* Relax in the wondrous assurance that I am *your Guide even to the end.*

Within your temple, O God, we meditate on your unfailing love. Like your name, O God, your praise reaches to the ends of the earth; your right hand is filled with righteousness. . . . For this God is our God for ever and ever; he will be our guide even to the end. —Psalm 48:9–10, 14

When Jacob awoke from his sleep, he thought, "Surely the LORD is in this place, and I was not aware of it." —Genesis 28:16

Be anxious for nothing, but in everything by prayer and supplication, with thanksgiving, let your requests be made known to God; and the peace of God, which surpasses all understanding, will guard your hearts and minds through Christ Jesus. —Philippians 4:6–7 NKJV

102

I AM TAKING CARE OF YOU. I know how hard this is to believe when conditions that are troubling you get worse instead of better. It's easy to feel as if I am letting you down—as if I really don't care about what you're going through. You know I could instantly change your circumstances, and you can't understand why I seem to be so unresponsive to your prayers. But I repeat: I *am* taking care of you.

To become aware of My loving Presence, you need to relax and stop trying to control things. Give up your futile efforts to think your way through your problems. Fall back into My strong arms with a sigh of trust. *Cease striving* and simply enjoy being in My Presence. Though there are many things you don't understand, you can rest in My unfailing Love. This Love is independent of all circumstances, and it will never be taken away from you.

Although My ways may be mysterious and unfathomable, My Love is perfect and everlasting. *Watch in hope for Me*, remembering that I am *God your Savior*.

Humble yourselves under the mighty hand of God, that He may exalt you in due time, casting all your care upon Him, for He cares for you. —1 Peter 5:6–7 NKJV

Cease striving and know that I am God; I will be exalted among the nations, I will be exalted in the earth. —Psalm 46:10 NASB

And [the Lord] said, "My presence will go with you, and I will give you rest." —Exodus 33:14 NKJV

As for me, I watch in hope for the Lord, I wait for God my Savior; my God will hear me. —Micah 7:7

Do not look to
your hope, but to
Christ, the source
of your hope.

CHARLES SPURGEON

Blessed is the man who trusts in the Lord, whose confidence is in him. He will be like a tree planted by the water that sends out its roots by the stream. It does not fear when heat comes; its leaves are always green. It has no worries in a year of drought and never fails to bear fruit.

JEREMIAH 17:7–8

103

You can *REJOICE IN YOUR SUFFERINGS* because you know that *suffering produces perseverance; perseverance, character; and character, hope.* Problems that cause you pain can ultimately increase your hope. However, this doesn't happen automatically. You have to cooperate with My Spirit as He guides you through times of suffering.

Perseverance is a rare commodity in this day and age. Most people look for and long for a quick fix. But lingering adversity—accepted with trust and confidence in Me—develops Christlike character. This prepares you for an eternity of problem-free living with Me. Your changed character will bless you and others in *this* world also, because I crafted you in My own image—to be like Me.

The more you become like Me, the more you can experience hope. Your transformed character convinces you that you do indeed belong to Me. This helps you cope with the problems you face, trusting that you and I *together* can handle them. And the wondrous hope of heaven shines on you daily, strengthening and encouraging you.

We also rejoice in our sufferings, because we know that suffering produces perseverance; perseverance, character; and character, hope. And hope does not disappoint us, because God has poured out his love into our hearts by the Holy Spirit, whom he has given us. —Romans 5:3–5

"If you love Me, keep My commandments. And I will pray the Father, and He will give you another Helper, that He may abide in you forever—the Spirit of truth, whom the world cannot receive, because it neither sees Him nor knows Him; but you know Him, for He dwells with you and will be in you." —John 14:15–17 NKJV

I can do all things through Christ who strengthens me. —Philippians 4:13 NKJV

104

LAY DOWN YOUR PROBLEMS long enough to gaze at Me. Picture yourself standing at the edge of an ocean, on a beach covered with pebbles. The pebbles represent problems—yours, your family's, your friends', the world's. As you pick up these small stones and hold them close to your eyes—examining their details—they obscure your view of the grandeur all around you. Usually, as soon as you put down one pebble-problem, you pick up another. Thus, you fail to enjoy the beauty of My Presence and to receive My help.

The ocean represents *Me*—endlessly glorious and continually present with you. I am calling you to put down all the pebbles for a time so that you can experience My Presence and receive *My unfailing Love*. Draw near Me by praying, "I choose *You*, Jesus. I choose to see You—to find You—in this moment." Practice doing this until it becomes a habit: a delightful habit that will keep you close to Me on *the path of Life*.

*Holy brothers, who share in the
heavenly calling, fix your thoughts
on Jesus, the apostle and high priest
whom we confess. —Hebrews 3:1*

*The LORD loves righteousness and justice; the
earth is full of his unfailing love. —Psalm 33:5*

*By faith [Moses] left Egypt, not fearing the
king's anger; he persevered because he saw
him who is invisible. —Hebrews 11:27*

*You will show me the path of life; in Your
presence is fullness of joy; at Your right hand
are pleasures forevermore. —Psalm 16:11 NKJV*

105

I AM IMMANUEL—*GOD WITH YOU*—and I am enough! When things in your life are flowing smoothly, it is easy to trust in My sufficiency. However, when you encounter rough patches—one after another after another—you may sometimes feel that My provision is inadequate. This is when your mind tends to go into high gear: obsessing about ways to make things better. There is nothing wrong with seeking solutions, but problem-solving can turn into an addiction: your mind spinning with so many plans and possibilities that you become confused and exhausted.

To protect yourself from this mental exhaustion, you need to remind yourself that *I am with you always*, taking care of you. It is possible to *rejoice in Me*—to proclaim My sufficiency—even during the most difficult times. This is a supernatural work, empowered by My Spirit who lives in you. It is also a decision that you make—day by day and moment by moment. Choose to *be joyful in Me, your Savior*, for I am indeed enough!

"She will bring forth a Son, and you shall call His name JESUS, for He will save His people from their sins." So all this was done that it might be fulfilled which was spoken by the Lord through the prophet, saying: "Behold, the virgin shall be with child, and bear a Son, and they shall call His name Immanuel," which is translated, "God with us." —Matthew 1:21–23 NKJV

"[Go and make disciples,] teaching them to obey everything I have commanded you. And surely I am with you always, to the very end of the age." —Matthew 28:20

Though the fig tree does not bud and there are no grapes on the vines, though the olive crop fails and the fields produce no food, though there are no sheep in the pen and no cattle in the stalls, yet I will rejoice in the LORD, I will be joyful in God my Savior. —Habakkuk 3:17–18

106

TAKE HOLD OF THE HOPE THAT I OFFER TO YOU—
and *be greatly encouraged.* The hope of heaven is your
birthright as a Christian. Many, many blessings flow
out of that glorious promise into your present life in
this world. Notice, however, that *take hold* is an active
verb—requiring effort on your part. As the apostle Paul
taught, you need to *press on toward the goal* and *live up
to what you have already attained.* This requires you to
exert yourself—grasping onto the heavenly hope from
which so many blessings flow.

One of those blessings is encouragement. *Be
encouraged* is a passive form of the verb. You receive
encouragement as a free gift from Me when you make
the effort to hold on to your hope—focusing on what I've
already done (died for your sins), what I *am* doing (living
in you), and what I *will* do (take you home to heaven). I
love to give good gifts in generous proportions. So cling
to hope, beloved, and you will be *greatly* encouraged.

God [confirmed his promise to Abraham] so
that, by two unchangeable things in which it
is impossible for God to lie, we who have fled
to take hold of the hope offered to us may
be greatly encouraged. —Hebrews 6:18

I press on toward the goal to win the prize for
which God has called me heavenward in Christ
Jesus. All of us who are mature should take
such a view of things. And if on some point
you think differently, that too God will make
clear to you. Only let us live up to what we
have already attained. —Philippians 3:14–16

I have been crucified with Christ; it is no
longer I who live, but Christ lives in me; and
the life which I now live in the flesh I live by
faith in the Son of God, who loved me and
gave Himself for me. —Galatians 2:20 NKJV

107

I ENABLE YOU TO GO ON THE HEIGHTS, to wander with Me in the Glory of My Presence. You may feel as if you can barely take the next step on this long journey upward. As you look ahead, you see cliffs that seem impossible for you to climb. *Yet I am with you always, holding you by your right hand. I guide you with My counsel,* helping you find the best way to scale those heights.

Though you are on a challenging—at times, grueling—journey with Me, it is much more than an endurance contest. The fact that I am with you can infuse Joy into the steepest climb! Be on the lookout for all the pleasures I have prepared for you, and take time to enjoy your devoted Companion.

You may think that "the heights" refers to the very top of the mountain you are climbing. But if you stop and look back at how far up you have come, you'll realize you are already on a high place. So relax a bit and gaze lovingly at Me. The Glory of My Presence is all around you!

*The Sovereign L*ORD *is my strength; he makes my feet like the feet of a deer, he enables me to go on the heights. —Habakkuk 3:19*

I am always with you; you hold me by my right hand. You guide me with your counsel, and afterward you will take me into glory. —Psalm 73:23–24

*I saw the L*ORD *sitting on a throne, high and lifted up, and the train of His robe filled the temple. Above it stood seraphim; each one had six wings: with two he covered his face, with two he covered his feet, and with two he flew. And one cried to another and said: "Holy, holy, holy is the L*ORD *of hosts; the whole earth is full of His glory!" —Isaiah 6:1–3 NKJV*

108

FIND REST IN ME ALONE, DEAR ONE; your hope comes from Me. You have a restless mind. It skips and scampers about continually, rarely taking time to be still. Listen, and you will hear Me saying, *"Come to Me."* I am the only resting place for your mind that will truly satisfy and strengthen you. Take time—make time—to direct your thoughts to Me. Whisper My Name and wait in My sacred Presence. You are on *holy ground.* This provides refreshment not only for your mind but also for your soul.

True hope comes from Me. False hope comes from many sources, including persuasive advertising. Ask Me to give you discernment as you seek to walk along a hopeful path. Many voices call out to you: "This is the way!" Do not be deceived; learn to be wise and alert when you're trying to process all the information shouting at you. Break free from information overload by refocusing your thoughts on Me. As you rest in My peaceful Presence, true hope grows within you.

*Find rest, O my soul, in God alone; my
hope comes from him. —Psalm 62:5*

*"Come to me, all you who are weary and
burdened, and I will give you rest. Take my
yoke upon you and learn from me, for I am
gentle and humble in heart, and you will find
rest for your souls." —Matthew 11:28–29*

*Then Moses said, "I will now turn aside and see
this great sight, why the bush does not burn." So
when the LORD saw that he turned aside to look,
God called to him from the midst of the bush and
said, "Moses! Moses!" And [Moses] said, "Here I
am." Then [God] said, "Do not draw near this place.
Take your sandals off your feet, for the place where
you stand is holy ground." —Exodus 3:3–5 NKJV*

*"I send you out as sheep in the midst of
wolves. Therefore be wise as serpents and
harmless as doves." —Matthew 10:16 NKJV*

What an excellent
ground of hope and
confidence we have
when we reflect upon
these three things in
prayer—the Father's
love, the Son's merit
and the Spirit's power!

Thomas Manton

May the God of peace,
who through the blood
of the eternal covenant
brought back from the
dead our Lord Jesus,
that great Shepherd
of the sheep, equip
you with everything
good for doing his will,
and may he work in
us what is pleasing
to him, through Jesus
Christ, to whom be
glory for ever and ever.

HEBREWS 13:20–21

109

I HAVE DONE GREAT THINGS FOR YOU, so let Me fill you with Joy. Take ample time to ponder all I have done for you. Rejoice in My goodness and My greatness as you remember My marvelous deeds. Rest in My intimate Presence; relax in My *everlasting arms.* I long to fill you with Joy, but you must collaborate with Me in this process.

Do not be like a spoiled child on Christmas Day—hastily tearing open all the presents and then saying, "Is that all?" Every single day is a precious gift from Me! *Search for Me* within the boundaries of this day, and you will surely find Me. I am present not only in pleasant things but also in unwanted circumstances. My Joy is sufficient for all situations, and I adjust it according to your need. When things are going your way, My gladness intensifies your delight. When you encounter hard things, I give you a deep, bold Joy that clings to Me for help. Receiving My Joy requires not only time but also courage.

The LORD has done great things for us, and we are filled with joy. —Psalm 126:3

The eternal God is your refuge, and underneath are the everlasting arms. —Deuteronomy 33:27 NKJV

"You will seek Me and find Me, when you search for Me with all your heart." —Jeremiah 29:13 NKJV

In this you greatly rejoice, though now for a little while you may have had to suffer grief in all kinds of trials. These have come so that your faith—of greater worth than gold, which perishes even though refined by fire—may be proved genuine and may result in praise, glory and honor when Jesus Christ is revealed. Though you have not seen him, you love him; and even though you do not see him now, you believe in him and are filled with an inexpressible and glorious joy. —1 Peter 1:6–8

110

MY EYES ARE ON THOSE whose hope is in My unfailing Love. To enjoy abundant Life, it is essential for you to have hope. However, many people indulge in false hopes and find themselves increasingly disillusioned as the years go by. So I urge you to choose well the object of your hope. The best choice is: *My unfailing Love.* From the time you first trusted Me as Savior, nothing—including *death, life, things present or things to come—can separate you from this Love.*

When you follow My divine guidelines, you can enjoy the Peace of My Presence. I am everywhere and I see everything, but My eyes are *especially* on those who are putting their hope in Me. Such people are ever so precious to Me, and I watch over them vigilantly. This does not mean I shield them from all adversity. It means I bless them with My nearness in good times, in hard times—at all times.

So persevere in placing your hope in My perfect Love. Look up to Me in the midst of your moments, for My eyes are indeed on you!

*The eyes of the LORD are on those who
fear him, on those whose hope is in
his unfailing love.* —Psalm 33:18

*I am persuaded that neither death nor life,
nor angels nor principalities nor powers,
nor things present nor things to come, nor
height nor depth, nor any other created
thing, shall be able to separate us from
the love of God which is in Christ Jesus
our Lord.* —Romans 8:38–39 NKJV

*Now may the Lord of peace himself give you
peace at all times and in every way. The Lord
be with all of you.* —2 Thessalonians 3:16

111

YOU ARE A DELIGHT TO ME! I know you find it difficult to receive this blessing. It is based on the unconditional Love I have for all of My followers. I love you more than you can begin to imagine, so just relax in the Light of My Presence—and take time to soak in this luminous Love. Relax with Me and listen while I *rejoice over you with singing.*

Living in a fallen world is a constant challenge. There is brokenness all around you, as well as within you. Each moment, you can choose to focus on what is wrong or to *seek My Face* and enjoy My approval. Even in the midst of important activities, you can breathe this short prayer: "I seek *You,* Jesus."

Remember that My delight in you is based on My finished work on the cross. So don't fall into the trap of trying to earn My Love. Instead, live as the one you truly are—My beloved—and let your gratitude keep you close to Me, eager to follow wherever I lead. I delight in you!

The Lᴏʀᴅ your God is with you, he is mighty to save. He will take great delight in you, he will quiet you with his love, he will rejoice over you with singing. —Zephaniah 3:17

When You said, "Seek My face," my heart said to You, "Your face, Lᴏʀᴅ, I will seek." —Psalm 27:8 ɴᴋᴊᴠ

The Lord make His face to shine upon and enlighten you and be gracious (kind, merciful, and giving favor) to you; the Lord lift up His [approving] countenance upon you and give you peace (tranquility of heart and life continually). —Numbers 6:25–26 ᴀᴍᴘ

112

HOPE IN ME, FOR YOU WILL AGAIN PRAISE ME for the help of My Presence. Sometimes—especially when you are feeling downcast or disturbed—it is hard to continue hoping in Me. At such times it's important to remember that Christian hope is much more than a feeling. It is confidence in Me: who I am (your Savior-God) and what I have promised to do (receive you into eternal Glory).

The help of My Presence is a constant in your life, but you are not always receptive to it. I am training you to exercise your trust and hope in Me by praising Me regardless of your feelings. The day will come when you will spontaneously burst into songs of worship—joyously praising Me for My glorious Presence! However, when you rejoice in Me during times of sadness, a marvelous thing happens: Your words of hope and trust in Me lift you above your circumstances. This sets your feet on an upward path of gratitude—where your Joy increases step by step. This *sacrifice of praise* is most pleasing to Me!

Why are you in despair, O my soul? And why have you become disturbed within me? Hope in God, for I shall again praise Him for the help of His presence. —Psalm 42:5 NASB

You guide me with your counsel, and afterward you will receive me to glory. —Psalm 73:24 ESV

As servants of God we commend ourselves in every way: in great endurance, in troubles, hardships and distresses. . . . sorrowful, yet always rejoicing; poor, yet making many rich; having nothing, and yet possessing everything. —2 Corinthians 6:4, 10

Through Jesus, therefore, let us continually offer to God a sacrifice of praise—the fruit of lips that confess his name. —Hebrews 13:15

I am the Light that shines on in the darkness, for the darkness has never overpowered it—and it never will! When multiple problems are closing in on you, the Light of My Presence may seem like a dim memory. If you are feeling distant from Me, it's time for you to stop everything and *pour out your heart to Me.* Carve out some time and space to talk with Me about your problems and your feelings. Let Me help you carry your burdens and show you the way forward.

No matter how much darkness you see in the world around you, My Light continues to *shine on,* for it is infinitely more powerful! Because you are My child, this Light shines not only upon you but also within you. You live *in the midst of a crooked and perverse generation,* and this is the perfect backdrop for you to *shine as light in the world.* Take time to bask in My radiant Presence. Let My boundless energy recharge your strength so you can blaze boldly in the darkness around you.

The Light shines on in the darkness, for the darkness has never overpowered it [put it out or absorbed it or appropriated it, and is unreceptive to it]. —John 1:5 AMP

Trust in him at all times, O people; pour out your hearts to him, for God is our refuge. —Psalm 62:8

Do all things without complaining and disputing, that you may become blameless and harmless, children of God without fault in the midst of a crooked and perverse generation, among whom you shine as lights in the world. —Philippians 2:14–15 NKJV

114

MY WAYS ARE HIGHER THAN YOUR WAYS, and My thoughts than your thoughts—as the heavens are higher than the earth. People are always trying to diminish Me: to cut Me down to a god who is understandable and predictable. When these attempts fail, they often respond by judging Me or denying My very existence.

You are not immune to such struggles. *Leaning on your own understanding* is your strong inclination, and this mind-set dies hard. But the truth is, you can no more understand the infinite wisdom of My ways than you can create something out of nothing. I made people in My image, and I have gifted some of them with remarkable creativity. However, every human creation is formed from substances that I made when I spoke the world into existence.

Whenever you find yourself struggling to accept My ways with you or My ways with the world, stop and remember who I AM. Bow your mind and heart before My infinite intelligence, and worship Me—the mysterious, majestic, holy One who suffered and died for you.

Seek the LORD while he may be found; call on him while he is near. Let the wicked forsake his way and the evil man his thoughts. Let him turn to the LORD, and he will have mercy on him, and to our God, for he will freely pardon. "For my thoughts are not your thoughts, neither are your ways my ways," declares the LORD. "As the heavens are higher than the earth, so are my ways higher than your ways and my thoughts than your thoughts." —Isaiah 55:6–9

Trust in the LORD with all your heart and lean not on your own understanding. —Proverbs 3:5

God said, "Let there be light," and there was light. . . . And God said, "Let the water under the sky be gathered to one place, and let dry ground appear." And it was so. —Genesis 1:3, 9

Hope is not the
conviction that
something will
turn out well but
the certainty that
something makes
sense, regardless of
how it turns out.

VACLAV HAVEL

*Continue to work out
your salvation with
fear and trembling, for
it is God who works
in you to will and to
act according to his
good purpose. . . . that
you may become . . .
children of God
without fault in a
crooked and depraved
generation, in which
you shine like stars
in the universe.*

PHILIPPIANS 2:12–13, 15

115

MAKE ME YOUR PRIMARY FOCUS. I am all around you—constantly aware of you. I take note of all your thoughts and prayers. Many, many things vie for your attention, but do not let them crowd Me out. Directing your mind toward Me requires very little energy and is imperceptible to others. Yet the more often you do this, the more fully I can live in you and through you.

Remember that I am present with you each moment of your life, watching over you with perfect Love. In fact, *My unfailing Love surrounds the one who trusts in Me.* I am training you to be increasingly aware of My loving Presence, even when other things demand your attention. I want to be the constant in your life that provides stability and direction in an unpredictable environment. *Since I am the same yesterday, today, and forever,* I can be the fixed point that helps you stay on course as you make your way through this ever-changing world. As you keep redirecting your thoughts to Me, I show you the way forward—and *I give you My Peace.*

I lift up my eyes to the hills—where does my help come from? My help comes from the LORD, the Maker of heaven and earth. He will not let your foot slip—he who watches over you will not slumber. —Psalm 121:1–3

Many are the woes of the wicked, but the LORD's unfailing love surrounds the man who trusts in him. —Psalm 32:10

Jesus Christ is the same yesterday, today, and forever. —Hebrews 13:8 NKJV

"Peace I leave with you, My peace I give to you; not as the world gives do I give to you. Let not your heart be troubled, neither let it be afraid." —John 14:27 NKJV

116

I AM CALLING YOU TO LIVE JOYFULLY in the midst of your struggles. You yearn for a freer, more independent way of life than you're currently experiencing. You pray fervently—and then wait hopefully for the changes you desire. When I don't answer your prayers according to your will, you sometimes get discouraged. It's easy for you to feel as if you're doing something wrong—as if you're missing out on what is best for you. When you think that way, you are forgetting a most important truth: that I am *Sovereign*. I am in control, and I am taking care of you.

I want you to accept your dependent way of living as a gift from Me. Moreover, I want you to receive this gift *joyfully*—with a glad and thankful heart. Actually, nothing will lift you out of the doldrums faster than thanking and praising Me. And nothing will help you enjoy My Presence more delightfully! *Enter My gates with thanksgiving and My courts with praise.*

The Sovereign Lord comes with power,
and his arm rules for him. See, his
reward is with him, and his recompense
accompanies him. —Isaiah 40:10

Indeed, O man, who are you to reply
against God? Will the thing formed say to
him who formed it, "Why have you made
me like this?" —Romans 9:20 NKJV

Enter his gates with thanksgiving and his
courts with praise; give thanks to him and
praise his name. For the Lord is good and his
love endures forever; his faithfulness continues
through all generations. —Psalm 100:4–5

117

BY DAY I DIRECT MY LOVE; *at night My song is with you—* for I am *the God of your life.* Take heart, My child, knowing that I am in charge of everything in your life. During the day, I command My Love to bless you in countless ways! So be on the lookout for the many good things I place along your path. Ask My Spirit to open your eyes so that you can perceive and receive all these blessings. Do not be discouraged by the hard things you encounter, for this is part of living in a deeply fallen world.

Rejoice that *My song is with you* throughout the night as I lovingly watch over you. If you are wakeful, use this time to seek My Face and enjoy My peaceful Presence. A tender intimacy with Me can develop when you *remember Me on your bed—meditating on Me in the night watches.* Whether you are waking or sleeping, I am always present with you. For I am indeed *the God of your life!*

*By day the L*ORD *directs his love, at*
night his song is with me—a prayer to
the God of my life. —Psalm 42:8

Be self-controlled and alert. Your enemy the
devil prowls around like a roaring lion looking
for someone to devour. Resist him, standing
firm in the faith, because you know that your
brothers throughout the world are undergoing
the same kind of sufferings. —1 Peter 5:8–9

When I remember You on my bed, I meditate
on You in the night watches. Because
You have been my help, therefore in the
shadow of Your wings I will rejoice. My
soul follows close behind You; Your right
hand upholds me. —Psalm 63:6–8 NKJV

118

BE WILLING TO KEEP CLIMBING this high mountain with Me. Sometimes you look back nostalgically at a long-ago stage of your journey. You yearn for that easier, less complicated time in your life. But I want you to recognize it for what it was: a base camp. It was a time and place of preparation for the arduous adventure ahead of you.

The mountain you are climbing is exceedingly high; the top of it is hidden in clouds. So it's impossible for you to know how far up those heights you have come—and how far you have yet to go. However, the higher you go, the better view you have.

Although each day is a challenge and you often feel weary, take time to enjoy the magnificent scenery! This journey with Me is training you to see from a heavenly perspective that transcends your circumstances. The higher up the mountain you climb, the steeper and more challenging your path becomes—but the greater your adventure as well. Remember that the higher you go with Me, the closer you get to your ultimate goal—the heights of heaven!

Now after six days Jesus took Peter, James, and John his brother, led them up on a high mountain by themselves; and He was transfigured before them. His face shone like the sun, and His clothes became as white as the light. —Matthew 17:1–2 NKJV

The Lord God is my Strength, my personal bravery, and my invincible army; He makes my feet like hinds' feet and will make me to walk [not to stand still in terror, but to walk] and make [spiritual] progress upon my high places [of trouble, suffering, or responsibility]! —Habakkuk 3:19 AMP

Our citizenship is in heaven. And we eagerly await a Savior from there, the Lord Jesus Christ, who, by the power that enables him to bring everything under his control, will transform our lowly bodies so that they will be like his glorious body. —Philippians 3:20–21

275

I TURN YOUR DARKNESS INTO LIGHT. After all, *I am the Light of the world*, and I am both with you and within you. Every day, you encounter darkness in the world—and in your heart—but remember that *I have overcome the world*. You can choose to focus on hurtful, wrong things or to focus on Me—the brilliant Overcomer!

I am calling you to walk with Me along *the way of Peace*. I know that many things tug at your consciousness and you have very real responsibilities in your life. However, I am training you to turn your thoughts to Me more and more—enjoying My Presence in tough times as well as good times. You will not be able to do this perfectly, but you *can* make progress bit by bit. As you direct your attention to Me, I push back the darkness with My invincible Light! This is how you walk in *the way of Peace*. This is how *I turn your darkness into Light*.

*You are my lamp, O L*ORD*; the* L*ORD *turns my darkness into light.* —2 Samuel 22:29

Then Jesus spoke to them again, saying, "I am the light of the world. He who follows Me shall not walk in darkness, but have the light of life." —John 8:12 NKJV

"I have told you these things, so that in me you may have peace. In this world you will have trouble. But take heart! I have overcome the world." —John 16:33

"And you, [John the Baptist], will be called the prophet of the Highest; for you will go before the face of the Lord to prepare His ways. . . . [in order for Jesus] to give light to those who sit in darkness and the shadow of death, to guide our feet into the way of peace." —Luke 1:76, 79 NKJV

120

LEAN ON, TRUST IN, AND BE CONFIDENT IN ME. The more challenging your life circumstances, the more you need to affirm—and lean on—your confident trust in Me. During difficult times, your natural tendency is to rely heavily on your own understanding. However, your human understanding is not up to this task; it will fail you time and again.

You have every reason to *be confident in Me*. I am the Creator and Sustainer of the universe, and I am in charge of every aspect of your life. Because the world is in such a fallen condition, it may seem as if I'm not in control. I could end all suffering instantly—by destroying the earth and taking My children Home—but I am waiting *to bring many sons and daughters to Glory*.

So take heart as you live in this broken world, believing that My eternal purposes are being worked out through your difficulties. Your troubles are part of My majestic Master Plan, and they *are achieving an eternal Glory that far outweighs them all!*

Lean on, trust in, and be confident in the Lord with all your heart and mind and do not rely on your own insight or understanding. —Proverbs 3:5 AMP

It was fitting for Him, for whom are all things and by whom are all things, in bringing many sons to glory, to make the captain of their salvation perfect through sufferings. —Hebrews 2:10 NKJV

Our light and momentary troubles are achieving for us an eternal glory that far outweighs them all. —2 Corinthians 4:17

The cross is an expectant cross. . . . It's a symbol of hope, for God is on one side and all the people on the other side, and Christ Jesus . . . is between us to bring us together.

DAVID JEREMIAH

*He is able also to
save forever those
who draw near to
God through Him,
since He always lives
to make intercession
for them.*

HEBREWS 7:25 NASB

121

BE STILL, AND KNOW THAT I AM GOD. Your life has been tumultuous recently—full of change and new responsibilities. You have continued to spend time alone with Me, but you've found it hard to really *be still* and focus on Me. You need to set aside time for listening to Me—blocking out distractions and reconnecting with Me in the depths of your soul. Without this focused time in My Presence, your soul will become malnourished. Other people may not notice, but *you* can tell the difference. Of course, I notice the difference even before you do. I can see the neediness within you—needs that only *I* can meet.

As you pour yourself into listening to Me, I want you to experience My delight in you. I see you as you truly are: My beloved child, gloriously clothed in My righteousness. Open your arms and your heart—to receive My delight in full measure. The Light of My Love is shining upon you. Be still in this holy Light, resting in the assurance of *My unfailing Love.*

*Be still, and know that I am God; I will
be exalted among the nations, I will be
exalted in the earth! —Psalm 46:10* NKJV

*As for the saints who are in the land,
they are the glorious ones in whom
is all my delight. —Psalm 16:3*

I will greatly rejoice in the LORD, *my soul shall be
joyful in my God; for He has clothed me with the
garments of salvation, He has covered me with
the robe of righteousness, as a bridegroom decks
himself with ornaments, and as a bride adorns
herself with her jewels. —Isaiah 61:10* NKJV

*In your unfailing love you will lead the people you
have redeemed. In your strength you will guide
them to your holy dwelling. —Exodus 15:13*

122

I AM GOOD—A REFUGE IN TIMES OF TROUBLE. I care for those who trust in Me. Even though you inhabit a world full of trouble, I assure you that I am completely, 100 percent good! *I am light, and in Me there is no darkness at all.* Seek in Me the perfection you have longed for all your life.

Because of the brokenness of this world, you always need a refuge—but especially *in times of trouble.* When you are hurting, I yearn to shelter you in My powerful, loving Presence. So turn to Me in tough times, and you will find Me faithful.

Many of My children fail to receive My help during difficult times because they don't really trust Me. When adversity strikes, they either lash out angrily at Me or become so focused on their problems that they forget I am with them. An essential element of trusting Me is remembering My promise to *be with you always.* Trust in Me, My child, and I will take care of you.

The LORD is good, a refuge in times of trouble. He cares for those who trust in him. —Nahum 1:7

This is the message which we have heard from Him and declare to you, that God is light and in Him is no darkness at all. —1 John 1:5 NKJV

When I am afraid, I put my trust in you. —Psalm 56:3 ESV

"Go and make disciples of all nations, baptizing them in the name of the Father and of the Son and of the Holy Spirit, teaching them to obey everything I have commanded you. And surely I am with you always, to the very end of the age." —Matthew 28:19–20

123

ALL THINGS WERE CREATED BY ME: things in heaven and on earth, visible and invisible. I am your Creator as well as your Savior. Every breath you breathe is a gift from Me. So it's wise to begin each day thanking Me for the precious gift of life, regardless of how you are feeling. This act of thankfulness connects you with Me—your living Savior—and helps you find your way through the day.

In Me all things hold together. Your life often feels fragmented, with many things pulling you this way and that. Your time and energy permit you to do only a small percentage of the possibilities that are beckoning you. So you need to set priorities and do the most important things first. I will help you with this as you stay in communication with Me. The more you bring your thoughts and plans to Me—seeking My guidance—the more effectively I can show you the way forward. Since *all things hold together in Me*, your life holds together better when there is more of Me in it!

By [Christ] all things were created: things in heaven and on earth, visible and invisible, whether thrones or powers or rulers or authorities; all things were created by him and for him. He is before all things, and in him all things hold together. —Colossians 1:16–17

I will instruct you and teach you in the way you should go; I will counsel you and watch over you. —Psalm 32:8

Let the morning bring me word of your unfailing love, for I have put my trust in you. Show me the way I should go, for to you I lift up my soul. —Psalm 143:8

124

REJOICE IN THE HOPE OF MY GLORY. Even though many people use the word *hope* to denote wishful thinking, My Glory-hope rings with the certainty of absolute truth! I have promised that all My children will share My Glory, and I intend to keep that promise. Moreover, I have all the Power I need—infinite Power—to enable Me to do so.

The nature of hope is that it refers to something in the future, something *not yet.* So you need to wait patiently for me to fulfill My promises. If patience is not your strong point, remember that it is a *fruit of the Spirit.* You can ask the Holy Spirit to help you wait hopefully in My Presence. Waiting is often a boring task unless you have something interesting to do *or* someone interesting to be with. When you wait in My Presence, rejoice that you are in the company of the Creator and Sustainer of the universe. I am infinitely more brilliant and creative than you can imagine. Delight in this awesome privilege of being with Me now and throughout eternity.

*We have peace with God through our Lord
Jesus Christ, through whom we have gained
access by faith into this grace in which
we now stand. And we rejoice in the hope
of the glory of God. —Romans 5:1–2*

*I consider that the sufferings of this present time
are not worthy to be compared with the glory
which shall be revealed in us. —Romans 8:18* NKJV

*The fruit of the Spirit is love, joy, peace,
patience, kindness, goodness, faithfulness,
gentleness, self-control; against such things
there is no law. —Galatians 5:22–23* NASB

Delight yourself in the LORD, *and he will give
you the desires of your heart. —Psalm 37:4* ESV

125

ENTER MY GATES WITH THANKSGIVING and My courts with praise. A thankful heart is a joyful heart, and this is what I want for you. When you neglect *the sacrifices of thanksgiving,* your soul suffers.

Many of My children who live in impoverished nations are more joyful than Christians in "rich" countries with material abundance. Even the greatest blessings can fail to bring Joy unless they are received with gratitude.

I am training you to thank Me not only for obvious blessings but also for situations you would never have chosen—a wayward child or spouse; loss of health, home, or employment. This is counterintuitive thankfulness, and it is possible only to the extent that you trust Me at a deep level. It is also a matter of self-discipline: willing yourself to thank Me even when your circumstances are screaming at you to find a way *out.* Though it is wise to look for ways to improve your situation, you cannot force My hand—or My timing. Just keep coming into My Presence with thanksgiving. Your persistent thankfulness may actually provide the long-awaited key I will use to unlock major difficulties in your life. *Giving thanks to Me* can open doors in ways that transcend your understanding.

Enter his gates with thanksgiving and his courts with praise; give thanks to him and praise his name. For the LORD is good and his love endures forever; his faithfulness continues through all generations. —Psalm 100:4–5

Oh, that men would give thanks to the LORD for His goodness, and for His wonderful works to the children of men! Let them sacrifice the sacrifices of thanksgiving, and declare His works with rejoicing. —Psalm 107:21–22 NKJV

"You now have sorrow; but I will see you again and your heart will rejoice, and your joy no one will take from you." —John 16:22 NKJV

126

Let My unfailing Love be your comfort. Something that brings you comfort should be dependable, and My Love will never fail you. My soothing Presence is always with you, but to receive the full benefits of this blessing, you need to trust Me wholeheartedly. Comfort is not only for your blessing but for your empowerment. When you feel secure in My Love, you are strengthened—and able to do the things I've prepared for you to do.

Love and comfort go together ever so naturally. When a small child needs comforting, the best remedy is often soothing words and a gentle kiss. Young children instinctively turn to their parents in such times of need, and you do well to learn from their example. When you are hurting, come to Me for comfort. Rest in Me, My child, and enjoy the gentle kiss of My Presence. Listen to Me as I *rejoice over you with singing.* To benefit fully from My comforting words, memorize scriptures that will assure you of My Love. Remember: I love you always—*with an everlasting Love.*

*May your unfailing love be my
comfort, according to your promise
to your servant.* —Psalm 119:76

*The LORD your God in your midst, the
Mighty One, will save; He will rejoice
over you with gladness, He will quiet you
with His love, He will rejoice over you
with singing.* —Zephaniah 3:17 NKJV

*The LORD has appeared of old to me, saying:
"Yes, I have loved you with an everlasting
love; therefore with lovingkindness I have
drawn you."* —Jeremiah 31:3 NKJV

Everything
that is done
in the world
is done by hope.

MARTIN LUTHER

*Now, Lord, for
what do I wait? My
hope is in You.*

PSALM 39:7 NASB

127

WATCH IN HOPE FOR ME. Wait for Me—your Savior; I will hear you. Your hope derives from the rock-solid fact that I am *God your Savior.* If I were only a human savior, my sacrificial life could not save you from your sins. If I were truly God but unwilling to become a human Redeemer, you would have no Savior. But since I am your Savior-God, you have every reason to *watch in hope!*

Look carefully for evidence of My working in your life circumstances. Do not grow weary in your waiting; trust that indeed *I will hear you.* In fact, I always hear your prayers—and also the Spirit's *intercession for you with groanings that cannot be uttered.* Believe that I am with you in the midst of your circumstances and that I am working on your behalf. Breathe in deep draughts of My calming Presence; fill yourself up with My Peace. Finally, find hope in thinking about who I AM: *I am He who will sustain you. I have made you and I will carry you; I will sustain you and I will rescue you.*

*As for me, I watch in hope for the
LORD, I wait for God my Savior; my
God will hear me.* —Micah 7:7

*The Spirit also helps in our weaknesses. For
we do not know what we should pray for
as we ought, but the Spirit Himself makes
intercession for us with groanings which
cannot be uttered.* —Romans 8:26 NKJV

*Even to your old age and gray hairs I am
he, I am he who will sustain you. I have
made you and I will carry you; I will sustain
you and I will rescue you.* —Isaiah 46:4

128

I GIVE STRENGTH TO THE WEARY and increase the power of the weak. You live in a world where weakness is often pitied—or even despised. People spend vast amounts of time, energy, and money on efforts to strengthen their bodies. They also use various stimulants to avoid or disguise weariness. However, weakness and weariness are simply part of the reality of living in a fallen world—and in a fallen body.

I invite you to come into My Presence confidently, with all your weariness and weakness. I have experiential understanding of fatigue because I lived in your world for thirty-three years. You can let down your guard with Me and admit how tired you really are.

Take time just to be with Me—basking in the Light of My Love. As *My Face shines upon you*, I bless you and *give you Peace.* Do not skimp on this time with Me, for I use it to strengthen you spiritually, emotionally, and physically. Lift up wide-open arms, seeking My Presence in the present moment. Be prepared to receive abundantly—Joy, Peace, *unfailing Love.*

*[The LORD] gives strength to the weary
and increases the power of the weak. Even
youths grow tired and weary, and young
men stumble and fall; but those who hope
in the LORD will renew their strength. They
will soar on wings like eagles; they will
run and not grow weary, they will walk
and not be faint. —Isaiah 40:29–31*

*The LORD make His face shine upon you,
and be gracious to you; the LORD lift
up His countenance upon you, and give
you peace. —Numbers 6:25–26 NKJV*

*Let your face shine on your servant; save
me in your unfailing love. —Psalm 31:16*

129

I AM THE ALPHA AND THE OMEGA, the Beginning and the End, who is and who was and who is to come, the Almighty. This planet you inhabit is in such a big mess that sometimes you feel overwhelmed. Just watching the news on television can make you anxious. World events and economies seem to be spinning out of control more and more. This is why it's so very important to focus on Me and consider who I am: *the Beginning and the End*. I—the Creator of this planet—transcend time. I know the end of this world's story just as well as I know its beginning.

I not only know how everything will turn out, but I am absolutely Sovereign. I am *the Almighty*; nothing is beyond My control. The more helpless you feel as you face the challenges in your life, the more comforting it is to trust that I am all-powerful. Remember that I am also compassionate. I am the Lord who *comforts His people and will have compassion on His afflicted ones.* You can transcend your troubles because I am both powerful and compassionate. So you have good reason to *rejoice*; sometimes you may even *burst into song*!

"I am the Alpha and the Omega, the Beginning and the End," says the Lord, "who is and who was and who is to come, the Almighty." —Revelation 1:8 NKJV

He who dwells in the shelter of the Most High will abide in the shadow of the Almighty. I will say to the LORD, *"My refuge and my fortress, my God, in whom I trust." —Psalm 91:1–2* ESV

Shout for joy, O heavens; rejoice, O earth; burst into song, O mountains! For the LORD *comforts his people and will have compassion on his afflicted ones. —Isaiah 49:13*

130

I AM ABLE TO DO IMMEASURABLY MORE than all you ask or imagine. So think big when you pray, but remember that I always think bigger! I am continually at work in your life, even when you can see nothing happening. It's easy for you to feel stuck in a situation you'd like to change because you can see only the present moment. But I look at the big picture—all the moments of your life—and I am doing more than you can imagine.

Try to stay in communication with Me as you go through this day. You can talk with Me about anything because I understand you perfectly. The easiest way to keep in touch is to begin each day with Me—bringing Me your praises and requests. Then, as you get into your activities, it's more natural to continue talking with Me.

The longer you wait to start communicating with Me, the more effort it will take. So come to Me early, before you get too far into your day. You may think you cannot spare the time for this, but remember that you don't handle things alone. You work collaboratively with the One who can do far *more than you ask or imagine.*

Now to him who is able to do immeasurably more than all we ask or imagine, according to his power that is at work within us. —Ephesians 3:20

The LORD reigns; he is robed in majesty; the LORD is robed; he has put on strength as his belt. Yes, the world is established; it shall never be moved. Your throne is established from of old; you are from everlasting. —Psalm 93:1–2 ESV

In the morning, O LORD, you hear my voice; in the morning I lay my requests before you and wait in expectation. —Psalm 5:3

131

HOPE AND COURAGE GO HAND IN HAND. When you are waiting, waiting, waiting for longed-for answers to prayer, it takes courage to continue hoping in Me. The world, the flesh, and the devil all tell you it's easier to just give up and give in to dull disappointment. In a sense, this is true. To keep praying with positive expectation requires a lot of effort and perseverance; giving up is *momentarily* easier. However, a resigned, I-give-up attitude is always hurtful in the long run. Often, this leads to cynicism—and eventually to despair. So it's well worth the effort to keep your hopefulness alive.

Courage comes from the French word for *heart*. Since I live in your heart, you can call upon Me to help you live courageously—facing adversity or danger with confidence and determination. I am well aware of your circumstances, and I take pleasure in helping you cope with them. So stand firm in My strength, beloved, refusing to give in or give up. I take pleasure in you always, but especially when you are bravely *hoping in My steadfast Love.*

Be strong and of good courage, do not fear nor be afraid of [the nations in the Promised Land]; for the LORD your God, He is the One who goes with you. He will not leave you nor forsake you. —Deuteronomy 31:6 NKJV

I pray also that the eyes of your heart may be enlightened in order that you may know the hope to which he has called you, the riches of his glorious inheritance in the saints, and his incomparably great power for us who believe. —Ephesians 1:18–19

The LORD takes pleasure in those who fear him, in those who hope in his steadfast love. —Psalm 147:11 ESV

132

YOU ARE HOLY AND BLAMELESS IN MY SIGHT. Let these words of blessing sink into your heart, mind, and spirit. You may find it hard to believe this amazing truth because you know that you fall short of My holy standard every single day. Indeed, you are not holy and blameless in yourself, and you will never be sinless in this life. Nonetheless, in *My* sight you are gloriously righteous. When you trusted Me as Savior, you gave Me all your sins—past, present, and future—and I gave you My perfect righteousness. This is an eternal exchange, securing your place in My royal family forever.

This was a most costly transaction for Me. Your *redemption, the forgiveness of sins*, was accomplished *through My blood*—poured out freely because I love you. I want you to ponder *how wide and long and high and deep* is this vast ocean of Love I have for you. As you spend time in My Presence—opening your heart to Me— you are able to receive more and more of *this Love that surpasses knowledge*!

[God] chose us in [Jesus] before the creation of the world to be holy and blameless in his sight. —Ephesians 1:4

In Him we have redemption through His blood, the forgiveness of sins, according to the riches of His grace. —Ephesians 1:7 NKJV

I pray that out of his glorious riches he may strengthen you with power through his Spirit in your inner being, so that Christ may dwell in your hearts through faith. And I pray that you, being rooted and established in love, may have power, together with all the saints, to grasp how wide and long and high and deep is the love of Christ, and to know this love that surpasses knowledge—that you may be filled to the measure of all the fullness of God. —Ephesians 3:16–19

On every page of the
Bible there are words
of God that give us
reason to hope. . . . In
the promises of God,
I find inspiration
and new hope.

CHARLES A. ALLEN

*Because of
his glory and
excellence, he has
given us great
and precious
promises. These
are the promises
that enable you
to share his
divine nature and
escape the world's
corruption caused
by human desires.*

2 PETER 1:4 NLT

133

HOLD UNSWERVINGLY TO THE HOPE YOU PROFESS, for I am faithful. Sometimes—especially when many things are going wrong—all you can do is hold on to Me. You would love to sort things out in your mind and find a way to go forward, but often this is impossible. The best thing to do at such times is *seek My Face* and *profess your hope.*

To profess hope is to affirm it openly. Your words matter! They make a difference, not only to other people but also to you. They have a strong influence on your physical and emotional well-being. Negative words will pull you down. But when you openly affirm your hope and trust in Me, you gain strength to move forward with confidence.

The basis of this confidence is that *I am faithful.* Moreover, *I will not let you be tempted beyond your ability* to endure. Sometimes *the way of escape* I provide is through your own words, such as: "I trust You, Jesus; my hope is in You." This sort of affirmation helps you hold on to your hope *unswervingly*—persistently.

*Let us hold unswervingly to the hope
we profess, for he who promised
is faithful. —Hebrews 10:23*

*Hear, O Lᴏʀᴅ, when I cry with my voice!
Have mercy also upon me, and answer
me. When You said, "Seek My face,"
my heart said to You, "Your face, Lᴏʀᴅ,
I will seek." —Psalm 27:7–8 ɴᴋᴊᴠ*

*No temptation has overtaken you that is
not common to man. God is faithful, and
he will not let you be tempted beyond your
ability, but with the temptation he will also
provide the way of escape, that you may be
able to endure it. —1 Corinthians 10:13 ᴇꜱᴠ*

134

I HAVE COME SO THAT YOU MAY HAVE LIFE—and have it more abundantly. The chief purpose of My incarnation was to secure eternal Life for you. However, I also want you to live abundantly *today*—and all your days. To do this, you need to remember Whose you are and who you are. You belong to Me, the Creator and Sustainer of the universe. And you are My beloved child, adopted into My royal family. Adoption is a forever-transaction: I have not hired you as My employee. I have made you a permanent member of My family.

Don't let the familiarity of these truths lull you into sleepwalking through your days. I, your faithful Guide, am more vibrantly alive than you can fathom! As you stay close to Me, some of My Life "rubs off" on you— awakening your heart so you can live more fully. This helps you see that you are on an adventurous journey with Me—where *you* make a difference, where your choices significantly impact the world. And *I, your God, will be your Guide even to the end.*

Then Jesus said to them again, "Most assuredly, I say to you, I am the door of the sheep. All who ever came before Me are thieves and robbers, but the sheep did not hear them. I am the door. If anyone enters by Me, he will be saved, and will go in and out and find pasture. The thief does not come except to steal, and to kill, and to destroy. I have come that they may have life, and that they may have it more abundantly." —John 10:7–10 NKJV

The Spirit Himself bears witness with our spirit that we are children of God. —Romans 8:16 NKJV

This God is our God for ever and ever; he will be our guide even to the end. —Psalm 48:14

YOUR LIGHT AND MOMENTARY TROUBLES are achieving for you an eternal Glory that far outweighs them all. The Greek word the apostle Paul used for *light* means "a weight-less trifle." Yet he had endured tremendous affliction: He had been imprisoned, beaten, and stoned—received thirty-nine lashes five times, was beaten with rods three times. He had been shipwrecked three times and spent a day and a night adrift at sea. He had often been hungry, thirsty, and cold. Yet Paul considered his massive troubles *a weightless trifle* because he was comparing them with *eternal Glory.* I am training you to view your problems this way too—from an eternal perspective.

I don't waste anything in your life, including your suffering. I use it to teach you important lessons here and now. But there is more. Your troubles are also accomplishing something in heavenly realms. They are *achieving eternal Glory*—contributing to the reward you will receive in heaven. However, for that to happen, you need to handle well the adversity in your life, trusting Me no matter what. When troubles are weighing you down, try to view them as momentary, weight-less trifles that are producing endless Glory!

Our light and momentary troubles are achieving for us an eternal glory that far outweighs them all. —2 Corinthians 4:17

From the Jews five times I received forty stripes minus one. Three times I was beaten with rods; once I was stoned; three times I was shipwrecked; a night and a day I have been in the deep; in journeys often, in perils of waters, in perils of robbers, in perils of my own countrymen, in perils of the Gentiles, in perils in the city, in perils in the wilderness, in perils in the sea, in perils among false brethren; in weariness and toil, in sleeplessness often, in hunger and thirst, in fastings often, in cold and nakedness. —2 Corinthians 11:24–27 NKJV

SET PRIORITIES IN YOUR LIFE ACCORDING TO MY WILL. You will not be able to do all the things you want to do—or all the things other people would like you to do. Setting priorities helps you make good decisions about what gets done and what does not.

Your time and energy are limited, so you may be able to accomplish only a small percentage of what you would like to do or feel that you "should" do. Therefore, *seek My Face* and My will as you look at the possibilities before you. Let biblical principles and promises guide you in determining what is most important.

Being intentional in this way will help you make the best use of your time and energy. It will also protect you from feeling anxious or guilty about all the things you are *not* doing. In order to do something well, you need to feel at peace about the many other things you could be doing—but are not. When you have set your priorities according to My will, you can relax and focus on accomplishing what *I* deem important. As you seek to please Me above all else, you will grow more and more into the *workmanship*—the masterpiece—I created you to be.

316

Seek the LORD and His strength; seek His face evermore! —Psalm 105:4 NKJV

How sweet are your words to my taste, sweeter than honey to my mouth! I gain understanding from your precepts; therefore I hate every wrong path. Your word is a lamp to my feet and a light for my path. —Psalm 119:103–105

We are His workmanship, created in Christ Jesus for good works, which God prepared beforehand that we should walk in them. —Ephesians 2:10 NKJV

137

I BROUGHT YOU OUT INTO A SPACIOUS PLACE; I rescued you because I delighted in you. No matter what your circumstances, if you belong to Me, you are in *a spacious place* of salvation. You may be feeling cramped in your current situation, but your salvation is an ever-expanding gift. My Spirit lives inside you, and He is always working to sanctify you—making you more like Me. This is an inner expansion, and it will continue till I call you home *to Glory*.

Heaven is a wondrously spacious place; you will never feel cramped or frustrated there. *I will wipe away every tear* from the eyes of My people. There will be *no more death, nor sorrow, nor crying*, and *no more pain*. Everything and everyone in heaven will be perfect. My limitless ocean of Love will wash over you and fill you to overflowing. You will finally be able to love Me—and other people—with perfect Love untainted by sin. This heavenly experience will continue to expand in ever-increasing gladness throughout eternity!

He brought me out into a spacious place; he rescued me because he delighted in me. —2 Samuel 22:20

You guide me with your counsel, and afterward you will receive me to glory. —Psalm 73:24 ESV

And I heard a loud voice from heaven saying, "Behold, the tabernacle of God is with men, and He will dwell with them, and they shall be His people. God Himself will be with them and be their God. And God will wipe away every tear from their eyes; there shall be no more death, nor sorrow, nor crying. There shall be no more pain, for the former things have passed away." —Revelation 21:3–4 NKJV

319

138

I am God your Savior. I guide you and teach you, so put *your hope in Me all day long.* I guide you according to *My truth*, and I teach you important lessons as you follow the path I've prepared for you. Because I am both your Savior and your God, I'm able to help you with the obstacles you will encounter. Your difficulties can even be blessings when they draw you into deeper dependence on Me.

It is important to have *your hope in Me all day long.* It's easy to be confident and trusting *sometimes*—when you are well rested and things are going smoothly. However, when things get hectic or unpleasant, you often forget the object of your hope: *Me.* Yet this is when you need Me the most! So make it your goal to keep your eyes on Me *all day long.* You won't be able to do this perfectly, but it is a worthy goal—one that gives focus to your thoughts. It also helps you enjoy My Presence as you go along *the path of Life.*

Guide me in your truth and teach me,
for you are God my Savior, and my hope
is in you all day long. —Psalm 25:5

Count it all joy, my brothers, when you meet
trials of various kinds. —James 1:2 ESV

I have set the LORD always before me;
because He is at my right hand I shall not
be moved. Therefore my heart is glad,
and my glory rejoices; my flesh also will
rest in hope. . . . You will show me the
path of life; in Your presence is fullness
of joy; at Your right hand are pleasures
forevermore. —Psalm 16:8–9, 11 NKJV

The future is
as bright as the
promises of God.

ADONIRAM JUDSON

The path of the righteous is like the first gleam of dawn, shining ever brighter till the full light of day.

PROVERBS 4:18

139

CAST ALL YOUR CARE ON ME, for I am watching over you. I am actually a very good Catcher, so throw Me your cares—your anxieties and concerns—with abandon. As soon as you release those worrisome things, you can breathe a sigh of relief and refresh yourself in My loving Presence. It doesn't matter if you have to do this many times each day—and sometimes during the night too. I am always awake, ready to catch your cares and bear your burdens.

Because I am infinitely powerful, bearing your burdens does not weigh Me down at all. In fact, I enjoy this game of catch very much because I see your load becoming lighter and your face becoming brighter. No matter how much you throw at Me, I never miss! So refuse to let your worries weigh you down. Remember that I am with you—ready to help with whatever you are facing. Instead of mulling over your problems, look to Me lightheartedly and say, "Catch, Jesus!" Then fling your cares into My strong, waiting hands.

[Cast] all your care upon Him, for He cares for you. —1 Peter 5:7 NKJV

Search me, O God, and know my heart; try me, and know my anxieties. —Psalm 139:23 NKJV

The LORD watches over you—the LORD is your shade at your right hand; the sun will not harm you by day, nor the moon by night. The LORD will keep you from all harm— he will watch over your life; the LORD will watch over your coming and going both now and forevermore. —Psalm 121:5–8

Praise be to the Lord, to God our Savior, who daily bears our burdens. —Psalm 68:19

140

SOMETIMES YOUR JOURNEY through this world is wearisome. You feel as if you've been plodding uphill wearing leaden clothing, and you don't want to take another step. At such times you need to stop and re-center your thoughts on Me. Remember that I am your constant Companion, eager to help you take the next step—and then the next. You have to take only one at a time! Instead of staring grimly into the future, dreading the journey ahead of you, direct your focus to the present and to My Presence with you.

As you walk with Me along your life-path, let the hope of heaven shine brightly on you, lighting up your perspective dramatically. Though the way ahead may be steep and difficult, the end of your journey is stunningly glorious—beyond description! And every moment you are getting closer to your heavenly home. As you look to Me in faith—trusting in My finished work on the cross— the Light of heaven's hope shines upon you and brightens the path just before you.

"Come to me, all you who are weary and burdened, and I will give you rest." —Matthew 11:28

❧

For we were saved in this hope, but hope that is seen is not hope; for why does one still hope for what he sees? But if we hope for what we do not see, we eagerly wait for it with perseverance. —Romans 8:24–25 NKJV

❧

The Lord will rescue me from every evil deed and bring me safely into his heavenly kingdom. To him be the glory forever and ever. —2 Timothy 4:18 ESV

❧

Blessed are those who have learned to acclaim you, who walk in the light of your presence, O LORD. *—Psalm 89:15*

141

MY WAYS ARE VERY MYSTERIOUS at times, even to those who know Me intimately. It's tempting for My followers to try to control the circumstances of their lives by being good enough. They may not even realize this is motivating their behavior. But when circumstances come crashing down around them—sometimes in tragic ways—they may feel as if I have let them down.

You must leave room for *mystery* in your worldview—accepting the limitations of your understanding and knowledge. I will never be predictable or controllable, but I am trustworthy. When adversity strikes you or your loved ones, remember the words of Job: "The LORD gave, and the LORD has taken away; blessed be the name of the LORD."

Though Job faltered at times during his excruciating ordeal, at the end of it he confessed, "Surely I spoke of things I did not understand, things too wonderful for me to know." Likewise, I urge you to view matters you cannot understand as divine mysteries: *things too wonderful for you to know.*

Beyond all question, the mystery of godliness is great: He appeared in a body, was vindicated by the Spirit, was seen by angels, was preached among the nations, was believed on in the world, was taken up in glory. —1 Timothy 3:16

Then Job arose, tore his robe, and shaved his head; and he fell to the ground and worshiped. And he said: "Naked I came from my mother's womb, and naked shall I return there. The Lord gave, and the Lord has taken away; blessed be the name of the Lord." In all this Job did not sin nor charge God with wrong. —Job 1:20–22 NKJV

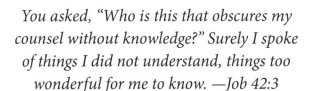

You asked, "Who is this that obscures my counsel without knowledge?" Surely I spoke of things I did not understand, things too wonderful for me to know. —Job 42:3

142

I am as near as a whispered prayer: listening attentively even to your softest utterance. People who are in love like to be near each other—usually as close as possible. Often they whisper words of endearment to each other, words that no one else can hear. This sort of closeness, with hushed words of love, is always available to you in your relationship with Me. *I am near to all who call on Me*, even if your call is the faintest whisper. This promise is for *all who call on Me in truth*—who know Me as *the Truth*.

Of course, I respond also to silent prayers, but whispering your words can help you feel closer to Me. Hearing your own voice—however faintly—reinforces your connection with Me. It strengthens your awareness of My unseen Presence and draws you into My loving embrace. Although I rarely speak audibly to My children, you can hear My gentle whispers in your heart. Hear Me saying, "I am with you. I love you. *I will never leave you or forsake you.*"

The LORD is near to all who call on him, to all who call on him in truth. —Psalm 145:18

Jesus said to [Thomas], "I am the way, the truth, and the life. No one comes to the Father except through Me." —John 14:6 NKJV

No one will be able to stand up against you all the days of your life. As I was with Moses, so I will be with you; I will never leave you nor forsake you. —Joshua 1:5

The LORD said, "Go out and stand on the mountain in the presence of the LORD, for the LORD is about to pass by." Then a great and powerful wind tore the mountains apart and shattered the rocks before the LORD, but the LORD was not in the wind. After the wind there was an earthquake, but the LORD was not in the earthquake. After the earthquake came a fire, but the LORD was not in the fire. And after the fire came a gentle whisper. —1 Kings 19:11–12

143

DIRECT YOUR THOUGHTS TO ME more and more. When you are working on a challenging project, you tend to seek My Face and My help frequently. This pleases Me—and it enhances the work you are doing. There is a delightful rhythm about this: You look to Me in a listening mode; then you act with the help of My Spirit. This is repeated over and over as you and I collaborate on the project. Being attentive to Me takes sustained effort, but this collaborative way of doing things does not drain you.

I encourage you to live more and more of your life in this way. When the task before you is less challenging, you tend to be less attentive to Me. You may even forget about Me for a while as your mind slips toward neutral. You forget that you live in a world at war—with an enemy that never rests. This is why the apostle Paul admonishes Christians to *be alert and always keep on praying*.

The more you direct your thoughts to Me, the more alive you will feel. This prayer-privilege is not a chore. It's a joyous lifeline!

Glory in his holy name; let the hearts of those who seek the LORD rejoice! —Psalm 105:3 ESV

"My sheep listen to my voice; I know them, and they follow me. I give them eternal life, and they shall never perish; no one can snatch them out of my hand." —John 10:27–28

A cloud overshadowed them, and a voice came out of the cloud, "This is my beloved Son; listen to him." And suddenly, looking around, they no longer saw anyone with them but Jesus only. —Mark 9:7–8 ESV

Pray in the Spirit on all occasions with all kinds of prayers and requests. With this in mind, be alert and always keep on praying for all the saints. —Ephesians 6:18

144

BE SELF-CONTROLLED—*putting on faith and love as a breastplate, and the hope of salvation as a helmet.* Self-control definitely involves struggle as you exert your will to abstain from ungodly behavior. Nonetheless, there is abundant help available to you in this battle. My Spirit, who lives within you, is your Helper. And *the fruit of the Spirit is love . . . self-control.*

A breastplate is designed to protect your heart and other vital organs when you are in battle. *Faith and love* combine to make an exceptionally effective breastplate. Your faith in Me, your Savior, enables you to trust in My righteousness, which is yours now and always. Love is the essence of My redeeming relationship with you. *The hope of salvation* makes a wonderful helmet because it protects your mind and reminds you that you belong to Me forever.

Faith, hope, and love all work together to shield you as you journey through this world. They also keep you close to Me.

Since we belong to the day, let us be self-controlled, putting on faith and love as a breastplate, and the hope of salvation as a helmet. —1 Thessalonians 5:8

The fruit of the Spirit is love, joy, peace, longsuffering, kindness, goodness, faithfulness, gentleness, self-control. Against such there is no law. —Galatians 5:22–23 NKJV

Stand therefore, having fastened on the belt of truth, and having put on the breastplate of righteousness, and, as shoes for your feet, having put on the readiness given by the gospel of peace. —Ephesians 6:14–15 ESV

Now these three remain: faith, hope and love. But the greatest of these is love. —1 Corinthians 13:13

I am training you to
hold in your heart
a dual focus: My
continual Presence and
the hope of heaven.

Jesus Calling

*Therefore, prepare
your minds for action;
be self-controlled;
set your hope fully
on the grace to be
given you when Jesus
Christ is revealed.*

1 Peter 1:13

145

BE OF GOOD COURAGE, *and I will strengthen your heart.*
I want you to face adversity with confidence and firm
determination. Because I am with you and the Holy Spirit
lives in you, you have everything you need to be bold.
Cowardliness is not of My kingdom. When you are feeling overwhelmed by your circumstances, remember who
you are—a child of the eternal King! Invite Me into the
very circumstances that are intimidating you, and let the
Light of My powerful Presence strengthen you. When you
choose to live courageously, I am pleased. And I respond
by strengthening your heart, thus increasing your valor.

Expect to encounter hardships as you journey toward
heaven because you live in a very broken world. This is
why bravery is desperately needed among My followers. You also need hope. My promise to *strengthen your
heart* is for those who *hope in Me.* Courage and hope are
closely connected in My kingdom. So I urge you to *hold
on to your courage and your hope.* They are more precious
than gold!

*Be of good courage, and He shall
strengthen your heart, all you who hope
in the L*ORD*. —Psalm 31:24* NKJV

⁓

*For you did not receive the spirit of bondage
again to fear, but you received the Spirit of
adoption by whom we cry out, "Abba, Father."
The Spirit Himself bears witness with our spirit
that we are children of God, and if children, then
heirs—heirs of God and joint heirs with Christ,
if indeed we suffer with Him, that we may also
be glorified together. —Romans 8:15–17* NKJV

⁓

*Now to the King eternal, immortal,
invisible, the only God, be honor and glory
for ever and ever. —1 Timothy 1:17*

⁓

*Christ is faithful as a son over God's house. And
we are his house, if we hold on to our courage
and the hope of which we boast. —Hebrews 3:6*

146

MY PEACE IS A SOFT, SOOTHING PILLOW for your weary head. Pry your mind away from plans and problems so you can rest in My healing Presence. Whisper, "I trust You, Jesus," while you relax—body, mind, and soul—in My protective Presence. If anxious thoughts try to intrude, give them over to Me *with thanksgiving*. Be grateful that I understand everything about you and your circumstances; also, I love you eternally and take care of you continually. Instead of pondering your problems, let these precious truths renew your mind. They *will set you free*.

As you refresh yourself in My peaceful Presence—trusting and thanking Me—I go to work on your behalf. While you stay in communication with Me, I show you the way forward. I may open up a way that previously seemed blocked, or I may take you along a new path altogether. Remember that you are never alone in your struggles. You have a Helper who is infinitely powerful, tenderly loving, and wise beyond all understanding. So *rejoice!*

And He said, "My Presence will go with you,
and I will give you rest." —Exodus 33:14 NKJV

Rejoice in the Lord always. I will say it again: Rejoice!
Let your gentleness be evident to all. The Lord is near.
Do not be anxious about anything, but in everything,
by prayer and petition, with thanksgiving, present
your requests to God. And the peace of God, which
transcends all understanding, will guard your hearts
and your minds in Christ Jesus. —Philippians 4:4–7

Jesus said to the Jews who had believed him,
"If you abide in my word, you are truly my
disciples, and you will know the truth, and the
truth will set you free." —John 8:31–32 ESV

"But when the Helper comes, whom I shall send to you
from the Father, the Spirit of truth who proceeds from
the Father, He will testify of Me." —John 15:26 NKJV

147

WAITING IS AN INESCAPABLE PART OF LIFE in this world. One of the hardest times to wait is during the night, if you're having trouble sleeping. As the darkness drags on while you're watching for the first rays of sunlight, you can identify with *watchmen waiting for the morning*. However, no matter how long the night may feel, dawn eventually comes. Since I created an orderly world, you can count on the rising of the sun.

There is much to learn from this pattern of expectant waiting followed by the dawning of a new day. People who are struggling with long-term problems may feel as if their suffering will go on interminably. But for My children there is every reason to be hopeful, even while circumstances remain dark. Relief *will* come! I can change situations and relieve suffering in an instant. Moreover, each of My followers is on a pathway leading to heaven.

Just as the night sometimes seems terribly long, yet always ends in dawn, so your journey through this world—no matter how long and hard it seems—will definitely end in Glory!

I wait for the LORD, my soul waits, and in his word I put my hope. My soul waits for the Lord more than watchmen wait for the morning, more than watchmen wait for the morning. —Psalm 130:5–6

As for me, I will see Your face in righteousness; I shall be satisfied when I awake in Your likeness. —Psalm 17:15 NKJV

Now to Him who is able to do exceedingly abundantly above all that we ask or think, according to the power that works in us, to Him be glory in the church by Christ Jesus to all generations, forever and ever. —Ephesians 3:20–21 NKJV

The sun shall be no more your light by day, nor for brightness shall the moon give you light; but the LORD will be your everlasting light, and your God will be your glory. —Isaiah 60:19 ESV

148

My Word is living and powerful; it is a discerner of the thoughts and intents of the heart. Because Scripture is alive, active, and full of Power, it can touch hearts deeply and transform lives thoroughly. I have changed *your* life through the wonders of biblical truth. My Word is continually at work in you, transforming you in the depths of your being. The more Scripture you have in your mind and heart, the more readily I can mold you.

Growing in grace is all about transformation—becoming more like Me. I never change: *I am the same yesterday, today, and forever.* So you are the one who needs to change—to be molded increasingly into My likeness. This is a glorious adventure and an awesome privilege! Yet it is also painful at times. Change always involves some loss, and it can trigger anxiety. The remedy is to cling to My hand—walking with Me in trusting dependence along the path I've prepared for you. *My Word is a lamp to your feet and a light for your path.*

The word of God is living and powerful, and sharper than any two-edged sword, piercing even to the division of soul and spirit, and of joints and marrow, and is a discerner of the thoughts and intents of the heart. —Hebrews 4:12 NKJV

Jesus Christ is the same yesterday, today, and forever. —Hebrews 13:8 NKJV

Those God foreknew he also predestined to be conformed to the likeness of his Son, that he might be the firstborn among many brothers. —Romans 8:29

Your word is a lamp to my feet and a light for my path. —Psalm 119:105

149

IF YOU HAVE A PROBLEM that comes and goes over a long period of time, you may start dreading its recurrence. This reaction only makes matters worse. When the painful situation returns, you tend to feel tense and defeated. You begin to judge each day that this circumstance is present as a *bad day*. This is a hurtful, negative focus.

Let Me suggest a better way: When the problem is absent or minimal, rejoice and thank Me continually—as often as you can remember. If the problem is present, look to Me and affirm your trust in Me. Ask My Spirit to help you persevere and keep your focus on Me. In doing so, you connect a positive thing—trusting Me—with something you previously considered quite negative.

If you do this consistently, you will find you are in a win-win situation. More importantly, you will no longer be letting your circumstances dictate the quality of your life. *Rejoice and be glad-hearted continually. Be unceasing in prayer—praying perseveringly. Thank Me in everything—no matter what the circumstances may be.*

Be joyful in hope, patient in affliction,
faithful in prayer. —Romans 12:12

Be happy [in your faith] and rejoice and
be glad-hearted continually (always); be
unceasing in prayer [praying perseveringly];
thank [God] in everything [no matter what the
circumstances may be, be thankful and give
thanks], for this is the will of God for you [who
are] in Christ Jesus [the Revealer and Mediator
of that will]. —1 Thessalonians 5:16–18 AMP

Let me hear in the morning of your
steadfast love, for in you I trust. Make
me know the way I should go, for to you
I lift up my soul. —Psalm 143:8 ESV

150

I AM *CHRIST IN YOU, THE HOPE OF GLORY.* The Messiah—the Savior of the world—lives in *you!* This promise is for all who have faith in Me: I *dwell in your hearts through faith.* This amazing blessing is a work of My Spirit in your inner being. The more you trust Me, the more you can enjoy My indwelling Presence—and the more effectively I can live through you.

In a world that may seem increasingly hopeless, remember that I am *the hope of Glory.* This hope is ultimately about heaven, where you will live with Me forever. But the Light of heaven's Glory is so brilliant that some of its rays can reach you even in the present—no matter how dark your circumstances may appear. I am *the Light that shines on in the darkness, for the darkness has never overpowered it.* As you follow Me along your life-path, clothed in My righteousness, this Light *shines brighter and brighter until full day.*

God has chosen to make known among
the Gentiles the glorious riches of this
mystery, which is Christ in you, the
hope of glory. —Colossians 1:27

I pray that out of his glorious riches he may
strengthen you with power through his Spirit in
your inner being, so that Christ may dwell in
your hearts through faith. —Ephesians 3:16–17

The Light shines on in the darkness, for the
darkness has never overpowered it [put it out or
absorbed it or appropriated it]. —John 1:5 AMP

The path of the righteous is like the light of
dawn, which shines brighter and brighter
until full day. —Proverbs 4:18 ESV

Scripture Index

Sarah Young's devotional writings are personal reflections from her daily quiet time of Bible reading, praying, and writing in prayer journals. With sales of more than 14 million books worldwide, *Jesus Calling®* has appeared on all major bestseller lists. Sarah's writings include *Jesus Calling®*, *Jesus Today®*, *Jesus Lives*™, *Dear Jesus*, *Jesus Calling® for Little Ones*, *Jesus Calling® Bible Storybook*, *Jesus Calling®: 365 Devotions for Kids*, and *Peace in His Presence*—each encouraging readers in their journey toward intimacy with Christ. Sarah and her husband were missionaries in Japan and Australia for many years. They currently live in the United States.

Jesus Calling® was written to help people connect not only with Jesus, the living Word, but also with the Bible— the only infallible, inerrant Word of God. Sarah endeavors to keep her devotional writing consistent with that unchanging standard. Many readers have shared that Sarah's books have helped them grow to love God's Word. As Sarah states in the introduction to *Jesus Calling®*, "The devotions . . . are meant to be read slowly, preferably in a quiet place—with your Bible open."

Sarah is biblically conservative in her faith and reformed in her doctrine. She earned a master's degree in biblical studies and counseling from Covenant Theological Seminary in St. Louis. She is a member of the Presbyterian Church in America (PCA), where her husband, Stephen, is an ordained minister. Stephen and Sarah continue to be missionaries with Mission to the World, the PCA mission board.

Sarah spends a great deal of time in prayer, reading the Bible, and memorizing Scripture. She especially enjoys praying daily for readers of all her books.